For Prentiss —
     We hope you will
enjoy and then go to the
backroad and enjoy travel —
Happy Texan Trails !

          James & Linda

TOURING TEXAS TOWNS...

and some that ain't

TOURING TEXAS TOWNS...

and some that ain't

Tales of traveling the
backroads of Texas—
135,000 miles and smiles

by
James and Linda Jennings

Touring Texas Towns... and some that ain't

Published by
Texas Travels Press

ISBN 0-9723035-0-2 (hardcover)

For information about this publication write to: Texas Travels Press, 518 Chaps Drive, Heath, Texas, 75032, or E-mail at texastravelspress@msn.com

Printed in USA
First Edition, 2002
05 04 03 02   10 9 8 7 6 5 4 3 2 1

Produced by NK Associates

Contents

Contents

INTRODUCTION

We probably missed a ghost town or two. Some ghost towns are towns that aren't there. We found a ghost town in the Big Bend the other day, one we hadn't been to in our 135,000-plus mile journey across Texas. Even when the wind whistled up a dirt devil, I still had the feeling that Linda and I were the only living thing there. Yes, there may be a town that once was—but now ain't—that may have slipped by us, but for the most part, we think we visited every town in Texas over a course of 3 1/2 years.

When I was a young man doing rodeos (I earned my bucks as a public address announcer versus being a cowboy contestant), I'd head out to some rural area on a given Wednesday, Thursday, Friday or Saturday night—April through September—and I always traveled on the back roads. So when Linda and I got married, I took her on a series of one-day and two-day jaunts into jack rabbit country and she was soon hooked!

Even after traveling to every Texas town, Linda's still anxious to see even more of Texas. It's a way of life for us. When we get too busy and don't make it out for a day or two, it's kind of like we've missed a day of reading the Bible. We love the back roads of Texas. If you want to see Texas, get off the Interstate. Texas is found on the backroads. If you try it once, I know you'll like it.

Do it a second time, and you'll be hooked, too!

LINDA AND I STARTED OUR JOURNEY across Texas innocently enough. We took a West Texas trip to Muleshoe, in Bailey County, in July of 1994. Outside of Muleshoe, the county seat, we drove through such places as Baileyboro, Circle Back, Needmore and the Three Way community—not even listed in the *Texas Almanac*—and I mentioned to Linda, "Why don't we just go to every town in the state?" She looked at me like I had a little sunstroke. "You're kidding, right?" she gulped. "I'm serious," I said. I figure we already had a good start. And as they say, the rest is history.

In November of 1997, we finished the tour on a Sunday in Pawnee, Bee County, in South Texas, and Linda says to me, "James, let's celebrate with some champagne and have a toast." But I told her, "Number One, we don't drink, and we wouldn't drink champagne if we had it, and secondly, where are you going to buy champagne in Pawnee, Texas, on a Sunday—unless you know the local bootlegger?" So we did what we thought was the second-best thing to celebrate our accomplishment. We made a right turn, went 15 miles out of the way to Kenedy, over in Karnes County, and we split a Blizzard at the Dairy Queen.

It wasn't the first Dairy Queen we stopped at during our travels; we went to hundreds of them. Believe me, they are fountains of knowledge. Just sit down and talk to some of the old-timers and you'll know what I mean.

PEOPLE HAVE ASKED ME how many towns are there in Texas. I don't really know. I don't want to know. But Linda kept count, and she recorded something over 3,300. We have volumes of photographs from every one of them, facts and notes this high, and several million memories that will be with us forever.

People we met along the way were so excited about what we were doing. We'd stop at a Dairy Queen, or at the local cafe on the square, and the locals would come to our table and say "You folks don't live around here, do you?" What they really wanted to know was what we were doing. This was a once-in-a-lifetime experience that can't be equaled.

We didn't have a master plan. We didn't take on Texas in any particular order. We didn't have a certain route to travel. We'd go to West Texas, then once we got tired of the flat lands, we'd go to the Hill Country, then we'd make a change and go to the coast, then up to the Panhandle—much of it depended on how much time we had to travel.

I said we didn't have a plan, but we really did. We always focused on a county, and drove the entire county—every town, every community, every crook in the road—before we would go to another county. If we didn't do that, we'd get very confused. As you know, there are 254 counties in Texas.

IN OUR TRAVELS, we did not call the local chamber of commerce. We went into a town to see what we could see, to experience what we could experience, and take photos of what impressed us—and we were impressed a lot, because we took a lot of photographs. I figure 21,000 or more.

We took with us *The Roads of Texas*—now held together by about two pounds of Scotch tape—probably one of the best detailed map of roads, and some that aren't, that I've ever seen in my life. It has roads, alleys, lanes, cattle guards, landing strips, cemeteries, everything is all there. It was our $14.95 roadside "Bible." I drove, Linda sat in the right front seat as the navigator, and when I questioned where we were—you know, "Have you got us lost?"—she would say "No, James. Right up the road here, we're going to make a 90-degree right-hand turn, and we're going to hit a dirt road." Sure enough, we did.

Did we ever get lost? Linda says not, although we did have to back up one road a quarter of a mile because there was no room for our Suburban to turn around. But Linda knew where we were at all times.

AT EVERY LUNCHEON or dinner when we talk about our travels, people ask us, "Where's your book?" Well, it took us another 3 1/2 years to get our thoughts collected, to sort through boxes upon boxes of photos, and pages and pages of notes. And every time we talked with someone about helping us write about our travels, I think the magnitude of what we did, what we saw, simply boggled their mind—and no one seemed to be ready to jump in and take on our project.

For Linda and I, it's one thing to get comfortable in a Suburban and hit the road, and it's another to sit down at a desk and write. We're not comfortable doing that. Writing is a task that is as foreign to us as drinking champagne. But we knew we had an interesting story to tell. Linda had taken a zillion notes, and I had processed thousands of photographs. So we just *knew* that we would find the right person to help us tell it. It turned out to be an old friend.

Eddie Hughes, who now lives in Loveland, Colorado, loves to write, and loves to travel. He's a native Texan, a former staff writer and photographer for *The Dallas Morning News*, a long-time Texas public relations executive with Southwestern Bell, and now retired. The problem with retired folks like Eddie is that he is so busy doing his own travels and his own writings that we were afraid to ask him to help us with ours. But one day, Linda asked. And he agreed. And thus, at long last, this book. We are indebted to Eddie, who listened to our tales, then said: "You have just written your book. I don't need to change a word. This story is your story, and you both tell it so well. Just consider me as your typist."

It should be noted that Eddie Hughes is more than a typist. He knows Texas. He's traveled its back roads. He knows what makes Texas unique, and he knows what people want to read and experience through photography and the printed word. We are most grateful to him for the countless hours he's spent at his computer and listening to us ramble and recall more than 3 1/2 years and 135,000 miles and smiles of memories.

Linda and I are also grateful to Neal Kimmel of Neal Kimmel and Associates of Carrollton for his tireless effort and professional touch in layout, design and production of this book.

Now take a deep breath, sit back in your comfortable reading chair, and enjoy some of our experiences while touring every Texas town, and some that ain't. ✪

—James Jennings
August 1, 2002
Heath, Texas

Hopkins County Courthouse in Sulphur Springs.

County
Courthouses

When you travel Texas, you always think of courthouses. They represent some of the finest works of public architecture—not only in Texas but in the entire country. They have been featured in documentaries, in movies, on calendars, even on telephone book covers. There's even a popular poster showing a photo collage of current county courthouse in each of Texas' 254 counties. That poster hangs on my office wall at home.

Not surprising, a lot of people we've met claim to have visited all 254 county courthouses in this state, and that's all well and good. Of course, I tell them (jokingly) that's a good start, but there's more.

There are actually more than 254 county courthouses in Texas. We found that to be true by driving to more than just the county seat of each county. A surprising number of old courthouses in Texas aren't in the present county seat at all. There are several old courthouses that are no longer in use, and are some of the most interesting ones in the state to visit. More on those later.

Texas is full of historic courthouses. In fact, according to the National Trust of Historic Preservation, some 225 are 50 years or older—and 80 of them were built in the 1800's. A total of 86 courthouses are listed in the National Register of Historic Places,

From Linda's notes

Hopkins County — Sulphur Springs was once known as Bright Star, but changed its name due to the many springs in the area. ...County's oldest brick structure is the Atkins House, built in 1870, located in Heritage Park. ...Don't miss visiting Southwest Dairy Center, a real tribute to the dairy industry. And check out the old-time soda fountain. ...Just out of town is a historical marker about Confederate refugees in Texas, including Amanda Stone who fled the war and brought 90 slaves with her.

and 78 have been declared Texas Historical Landmarks.

Unfortunately, quite a few are falling into disrepair, and two—Hill County Courthouse in Hillsboro and Newton County in Newton—have burned just in the last decade. You hate to see these old icons of Texas history disappear from the landscape, or slowly fade into the sunset.

Many have asked us which courthouse is our favorite. There are many that could be in our Top 10 list—and it's possible my top 10 would be different from Linda's top 10. It's like looking at art. There is always something fascinating about the architecture of our courthouses, but there is also something unique that makes it stand out.

I GREW UP IN Hopkins County, and became quite familiar with our county's old courthouse in Sulphur Springs. I really never thought too much about that fine old Romanesque Revival-style relic, almost identical to the impressive red granite masterpieces in Ellis and Wise counties, all built in the early 1890s.

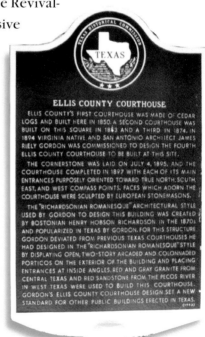

When we began to make our tour of Texas towns and counties, however, I was awe-struck by the beauty of "my" old courthouse in Hopkins County—much more beautiful than I ever knew it to be. Some of the photographs I took of that old courthouse are still among my favorites.

The Hopkins County courthouse may not be as "famous" as the "Grande Dame" Ellis County courthouse in Waxahachie, or the "perfect pink"

14

Ellis County Courthouse in Waxahachie is called the "Grande Dame" of courthouses.

limestone Wise County landmark in Decatur. But the Hopkins County courthouse is unique in that it doesn't sit in the middle of the town square like all of its Texas cousins. Rather, it sits on a corner of the downtown square. When I was growing up, I never knew that was a unique aspect of my old hometown courthouse.

NOW, I DON'T WANT TO TAKE AWAY the charm and beauty of many, many county courthouses in our state, nor what they meant to the history of Texas, but there are a lot of courthouses throughout our state that are no longer in use—or, at least, no longer being used as a courthouse per se. And two of our favorites are just 50 miles apart.

If you find yourself traveling down U.S. Hwy 67 south in the rolling hills of Irion County, near the

From
Linda's notes

Irion County — Big sheep country, but watch out for deer near Mertzon. Lots of deer on roads and around town ...Old Sherwood courthouse one of best examples of early-Texas courthouses, a mile north and a mile east of Mertzon. Still curious about painted hands on clock! ...Outlaw Tom Ketchum once maintained a hideout in the county, on a mountain (2,725 feet elevation) now named for him.

Old Irion County courthouse in Sherwood features painted hands on the clock tower.

present county seat of Mertzon, there's a sign—maybe a mile before you get to Mertzon—that shows Sherwood is two miles to the left. Take that turn, go less than two miles, and you will be shocked at the beauty of an old, old courthouse standing in downtown Sherwood.

Sherwood is a community of maybe 75 people. It used to be the county seat of Irion County, from 1889 until 1936. This old three-story structure with a bell tower still intact is one of the best examples of early-day Texas courthouses. Still surviving on the old grounds (now fenced in) are old hitching posts and watering troughs. The courthouse is closed, except for special occasions and festivals, and is owned and cared for by the Sherwood Community Association. A unique thing about the clock on the clock tower: It's hands are painted on the face of the clock. That was apparently a common occurrence on courthouses built in the 1880s.

JUST A FEW MILES DOWN U.S. 67 past Mertzon, you'll enter Reagan County and the current county seat at Big Lake. There's a feed store in town, where we stopped primarily to get some information on a cowboy I had spent some time with on the rodeo circuit. I learned, from a kind gentleman at the feed store, that my old cowboy friend was on an out-of-state trip, probably getting his neck broke. Turned out the fellow I was talking to was the county judge by the name of Mike Elkins.

I mentioned to Judge Elkins that we had heard about an old courthouse in the Reagan County community of Stiles, north of Big Lake, and asked if he knew anything about it. "Sure do," he said, "and further more, if you'll bring me back to town, I'll go with you to see that old courthouse, because I got the key to it."

We took the judge up on his offer and drove 20 miles up Texas Hwy. 137. I don't remember seeing a single ranch house along the

Old Reagan County courthouse in Stiles was built of stone from nearby quarry. (Inset below) Old boots found on the porch of the old Stiles courthouse.

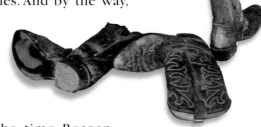

way, but we did see the old courthouse in Stiles long before we ever got to Stiles. And by the way, according to the *Texas Almanac*, Stiles has a population of 12. As far as I could tell, we were the only three there.

We learned that at the time Reagan County was formed, in 1903, Stiles was the only town in the county. An old wooden building served as its first courthouse, then the citizens of Reagan County passed a bond issue for $20,000 in 1911 to build a new one. As the result, this old classic two-story white limestone courthouse was built in only eight months from stone carved out of a quarry a half-mile away. Judge Elkins said the native stone of the old courthouse was hauled in by wagon drawn by a donkey and a mule.

Another interesting side-story is that among the locals who carted the stone to the town square was a stone mason by trade, who had just moved to the county. But he never worked on the courthouse, because he belonged to the Stone Masons Union, and the county powers voted to build their courthouse without union labor. History can have a rather ironic side.

Even more ironic is the fact that this courthouse was doomed from the start. A year after the courthouse was finished, Stiles' fate as the county seat hit a snag. We learned from the judge that the Kansas City, Mexico & Orient Railroad was building a line between San Angelo and Fort Stockton and intended the railroad to run through Stiles. But a prominent rancher in the area refused to allow the railroad to come through his property, so the rail line was moved 20 miles to the south, and Big Lake was born.

The rest, they say, is history. Thanks to the railroad and the

From
Linda's notes

Reagan County — Hickman Museum in Big Lake tells the story of how oil can change a community and a state. Santa Rita No. 1 gushed in a big oil pool that made the University of Texas one of the richest schools in the nation. Actual well site with derrick is four miles west of town on U.S. 67. ...Old county courthouse is on a ranch in Stiles, and the upper floor ballroom was worth the visit, even though it's now falling in.

Present Reagan County Courthouse was built in Big Lake when the railroad bypassed Stiles.

discovery of oil at Santa Rita No. 1 in 1923, Big Lake grew fast. As the result, a vote was taken in 1925 and, overwhelmingly, county voters—most of them living in Big Lake—voted to move the county seat to Big Lake and build another courthouse. And that was just about the end of Stiles and this old courthouse as a courthouse.

Thanks to the judge and his key to the front door, we got to tour the old courthouse in Stiles. Maybe we shouldn't have. It is really beginning to fall apart—the timbers are rotting and the floors are dangerous—and I don't know how much longer that old historic building will be left standing. It was used as a community center for several years, and as a school house for a year, but has been empty since the early 1950's. It was added as a Texas Historic Landmark in 1969—thus, well worth a visit and a photograph or two.

GEORGE WEST IS THE COUNTY SEAT of Live Oak County, but it wasn't always that way. The county seat used to be in Oakville.

From
Linda's notes

Live Oak County — Courthouse in George West has interesting museum. ...West Hotel Emporium is in a renovated 1919 hotel with cute gifts and remarkable antiques. The old Buck West House now houses the local chamber of commerce. ...One-half mile south of town is the Grace Armstrong Museum, with interesting collections of seashells, rocks, china and smoking pipes. ...Van's Bar-B-Que in Oakville sells cakes baked in Mason jars.

Today, Oakville is split right down the middle by Interstate Highway 37, that spans the coastal prairie between San Antonio and Corpus Christi. If you get off the interstate at Oakville, on the right side there's a small store with a post office that may be 120 or so years old. They are still using the mail boxes they used when the post office was opened.

From there, you drive over a bridge and cross the interstate. No doubt you'll run into a little place called Van's Barbecue. Good BBQ, by the way. It has an unusual coed bathroom with a bathtub, complete with a mannequin in the tub that will quickly get your attention. As we left to pay our bill, there was a small basket on the

Original Live Oak County courthouse in Oakville had it better days.

counter next to the cash register with a sign that said "Boneless Chicken. 50 cents." Now that immediately aroused my curiosity. So I had to try some. Which at Van's Barbecue, in Oakville, happens to be boiled eggs!

There is an old two-story stone building standing in Oakville. It's no more than five or six blocks from Van's Barbecue. It's not too hard to find, because it's the only multi-story building in the entire area. We were told that this structure once served as a county courthouse, though others say it was the old county jail for years. Suffice to say, the one-time county building has been closed for many years. It needs a lot of repair, and is not exactly attractive, with weeds and grass grown up all around.

We learned that the old courthouse/jail is actually owned by two brothers who don't speak to each other. That means these two brothers can't exactly agree on what to do with this old storied building, so it just sits there. That's really too bad, because it could be a great historic stop in the little town of Oakville.

ANOTHER UNUSUAL, one-time courthouse is in Stonewall County. Aspermont is now the county seat of Stonewall County, but the old, old county courthouse is several miles out of Aspermont, on U.S. Hwy

One-time Stonewall County courthouse near Aspermonte is now a ranch house, which also includes the old Rayner Cemetery.

380, and it is now a ranch house.

Stonewall County was formed out of the Bexar and Young land districts in 1876, and named after Confederate General Thomas J. "Stonewall" Jackson. But it was 12 years before it finally settled on where its county government would be located. A local rancher, W. E. Rayner, bought land for a town site and the community of Rayner was selected, and a courthouse building of native stone, complete with a cupola (now gone), was built. Unfortunately, Rayner didn't last long as the county seat.

After two years, a tug-of-war over records, deeds and other matters ensued, and Aspermont became the official county seat in 1898. The courthouse in Rayner was then purchased by a local rancher, including the property around it, and has been a private residence ever since. It was once known as the "Baldwin House." As we noted in the chapter on Old Cemeteries, this is the ranch that includes the old Rayner Cemetery.

UP IN THE PANHANDLE, Vega is the county seat of Oldham County, but in the early days, it was the town of Tascosa. Now a ghost town, Old Tascosa is today part of Cal Farley's Boys Ranch and the old courthouse that once served Oldham County is now the Julian Bivins Museum—named for the pioneer rancher who donated much of the land that formed the nucleus of the Boys Ranch.

From Linda's notes

Oldham County — Dr. Oscar Lloyd was a weather forecaster in Vega, and farmed with a steam engine. Donated his ranch to charitable institutions, including the Boys' Ranch. He was one of the founders of the Route 66 Association.

The Boys Ranch—the home for boys and girls in need of affection, discipline and education—is a great place to visit. It sits right on U.S. Hwy. 385, on the right if you're headed north toward Dalhart. The first boys who came to the ranch in the early 1940's actually lived in the old, abandoned courthouse of Tascosa. We talked a little about the ranch, and Old Tascosa's Boot Hill Cemetery in the cemeteries chapter.

One-time Oldham County courthouse in Tascosa (below) is now the Julian Bivins Museum, in honor of the rancher who donated land for Cal Farley's Boys Ranch.

The old courthouse-now-museum is open from 10 a.m. to 5 p.m. year round, and includes artifacts from Indian and prehistoric cultures, as well as cowboy and pioneer items, and photos depicting the history of the Boys Ranch that was started by the late Cal Farley in 1939.

IN THE TOWN OF CALVERT, Robertson County, many Victorian homes and businesses have historical medallions, making it one of Texas' most "Victorian" towns. It has two other claims to fame: it once bragged on having the largest cotton gin in the world, and it served as the county seat from 1870 to 1879. But in 1873, even before they could complete construction of the courthouse in Calvert, an epidemic of Yellow Fever took the lives of many

Robertson County's first courthouse in Calvert closed even before it was finished due to a Yellow Fever epidemic in the mid-1870's.

civic leaders. So they moved the county records to Franklin, and in 1879 they built a new courthouse and Franklin has been the county seat of Robertson County ever since. But the old county courthouse in Calvert still stands.

DID YOU KNOW there is a courthouse that isn't even in the town that is officially the county seat? That's the case in Bowie County.

Bowie County is the furthermost northeast county in Texas, bordered on the north by Oklahoma and on the east by Louisiana. Bowie County includes the border city of Texarkana, which straddles the Texas and Arkansas line.

Old Bowie County courthouse in Boston (upper photo) burned, and a new courthouse was built in 1986 in New Boston, which today is still not the official county seat.

The county seat of Bowie County is Boston. Now, that's not to be confused with New Boston, or even Old Boston. In truth, they are as close as cousins, and that is why the story of the Bowie County courthouse is so unique. It gets rather convoluted, but that is what makes Texas history so interesting.

In 1840, when the county was organized, it wanted the county seat to be in the center of the county, and that would be where Old Boston is now—only then, they tried to name it Center, but there were already three towns in Texas named Center, so it was named simply Boston. But then Texarkana folks (there were plenty of them even in 1840) got hold of the official county papers in 1841 and declared their city to be the county seat. That lasted until 1890, when

The historic Hill County Courthouse in Hillsboro underwent renovation after a fire.

that courthouse burned, along with all the county records. So they built another courthouse between what was then Boston, the original county seat site, and New Boston, which had become the county's new trading center.

So, the story goes, the new courthouse site became known as Boston, and the original Boston became Old Boston. And if you think the story ends there, hang on.

As New Boston grew in size, and Boston didn't, county leaders decided it would be best to build a new courthouse there, but keep Boston as its official county seat. And

The chateau-styled Newton County Courthouse in Newton, above and right, really glows during the Christmas season.

that's what they did in 1986. So the Bowie County Courthouse today is in New Boston, and the county seat is Boston.

You can still see the old courthouse building in Boston, even though it was torched by an arsonist in 1987, and is in bad shape. You can see the new county courthouse in New Boston, but remember— it is not the official county seat.✪

Paint Rock Methodist Church in Paint Rock, Concho County.

CHAPTER TWO

Country Churches

We could do a book on Texas country churches. If there was any one thing that inspired us most while traveling on the backroads of this state, it had to be the charming, often characteristically simple, and always community-focused, icons of rural Texas—the countless country churches that can be found at virtually every turn of the road.

Purposely, we have not included the big brick edifices or spire-inspired cathedrals that you find in the corporate city limits of every community, large and small. That *would* end up being a book! In this chapter, we will concentrate, instead, on those isolated chapels of backwoodsy inspiration.

As testimony of our devotion to country churches, we took more than 2,000 photographs. So you can see that this chapter will necessarily include only those quaint or unique churches that we can readily recall, or that speak of the simplicity of rural religious experience not only in the early days of Texas, and in many instances are still meeting the spiritual needs of Texas' faithful.

What often is missing, when you visit an old church on the back roads, is the story that could go with it. When we could, we visited with those who always had a story to tell about their church, and there were many—too many for this book.

Allison Chapel Methodist Church in Fair Play.

ONE OF OUR FAVORITE church stories—from one of the favorite people we met—was near Atlanta, in the piney woods and lake country of Cass County, in deep East Texas. It was the Laws Chapel Methodist Church, started by the Laws family well over 100 years ago, upgraded many times, and it is still a meeting place for the faithful.

When we pulled up in front of the church, we spotted some workers inside the building doing some repairs and spiffying up the already well-kept chapel. While we were reading the historical marker in front of the building, a very distinguished elderly man walked up to us, and introduced himself as being a church member and the one who helped oversee work being done on the church.

His name was W.T. Stamps, and he proudly noted that he had been a member of the Laws Chapel Methodist Church since he was 5 years

From
Linda's notes

Cass County—
Atlanta is truly a beautiful East Texas town, named because many of its settlers were from Georgia. Prehistoric Caddo Indian village sites are located throughout this area.

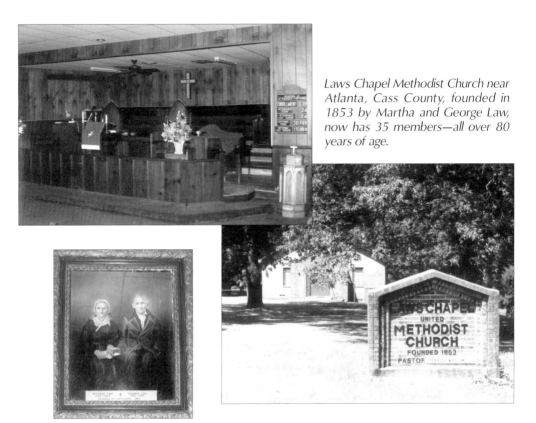

Laws Chapel Methodist Church near Atlanta, Cass County, founded in 1853 by Martha and George Law, now has 35 members—all over 80 years of age.

old. He was now 80 years of age. He said the church had 35 members, and he was—now get this—the *youngest* member of the congregation.

He took us on a tour of the church, proudly showing how they were keeping up the building, using members to do all the work, and not one of the volunteer workers was under 80 years of age. What a blessing this church has meant to those who worship here. Makes you wish that was true everywhere!

It was Mr. Stamps (even as the youngest member of the church, he deserves such reverence) who gave me a line that I have used time and again, as I think about getting older: "Laws Chapel Methodist Church," he said, "is having a lot more funerals now than weddings."

Speaking of church activity, in the little town of Tell, Childress

Two of three churches in Tell, Childress County, are still active. This one wasn't.

County, where even the cotton gin is closed, there are three church buildings—but only two were active, a Methodist and a Baptist church. The two churches are about three blocks apart. According to the Postmaster in Tell, the total membership between these two churches is 7. And both have Sunday services every Sunday. Ah, the spirit is alive and well in Tell, testimony of the role country churches play in the life of a community.

AN INTERESTING early-day Methodist church is McMahan's Chapel, near Hemphill, in Sabine County. It's about two miles off Hwy. 21, on an oil-topped road (Spur 35) that becomes a dirt road, in a beautiful setting among tall stands of shortleaf pine. This church was made of brick, a bit unusual for rural churches, especially in the heart of timber forests.

COUNTRY CHURCHES

The McMahan's Chapel Methodist Church is the oldest, continually-operated Methodist church in Texas. It became a church back in 1834, with the first building built in 1839, and it's been open 24 hours a day ever since. You're always welcome here to come for prayer, meditation, or just to gaze upon the beautiful stained glass windows that add to the church's aura of sacred stability.

The one really unusual thing about the McMahan's Chapel is its lectern. The church was originally organized by an evangelist by the name of Littleton Fowler. He was an early Texas Bible-totin' circuit rider, and he is buried under the pulpit of the first building which had a dirt floor. His tombstone today can be seen in front of the lectern in the McMahan's Chapel. That would make it hard for one to go to sleep during a service, don't you think?

Oldest and still-active Methodist church in Texas is the McMahan Chapel near Hemphill, Sabine County, founded in 1834.

SPEAKING OF CEMETERIES and tombstones reminds me of another rare find in our fascination with old country churches.

Driving west from San Antonio, on U.S. Hwy. 90, maybe eight miles from Hondo, we found Old D'Hanis, just a butterfly flit from D'Hanis, and there we came across St. Dominique Catholic Church, founded in 1847, when Texas was its own Republic. Now this old church hasn't been used in many years. There is no roof over the old limestone building, no windows, and a cemetery that joins the churchyard in the back.

Tombstones in the St. Dominic Catholic Church's Cemetery in Old D'Hanis, Medina County, are inscribed only in French and German.

Two things peaked our interest in the cemetery. One, all the writings on the tombstones are either in German or French. None are in English. And, secondly, there have been no burials in the cemetery since the 1890s.

Another interesting old Catholic church is in McFadden, Victoria County, just a couple of miles off U.S. Hwy 77, and about 20 miles south of Victoria, the county seat. The community of McFadden is actually part of the old McFadden Ranch, once one of Texas largest ranching operations. Not much ranching is going on now, but the church still stands, along with the old McFadden school, the post office, and a general store that operates a fairly decent restaurant just for the noon hour crowd.

The church in McFadden is known as the Infant Jesus of Prague Catholic Church, which was built by McFadden himself to serve those who worked on his ranch. The unusual thing about this old weather-beaten wood church is that it is said to be the only privately-owned Catholic church in the United States. That's what we were told by several people in the area, but we haven't taken the time to verify whether that is the case. But this is Texas, God's country, so I suspect we were told the gospel truth.

From
Linda's notes

McFadden Ranch — Helen Knebb, who helps her daughter Greta at the ranch store, says the McFadden Ranch had 180 workers who lived on the ranch. At one time, it had three schools, serving whites, Mexicans and blacks.

ANOTHER GOSPEL TRUTH is that you can find churches where nothing else exists. The best example of that is in Pumpville, way out on the edge of nowhere in Val Verde County. You won't find it on the official state map, but we came across it while traveling between Sanderson and Del Rio, following U.S.

The Infant Jesus of Prague Catholic Church in McFadden, Victoria County, claims to be the only "privately-owned" Catholic church in the U.S.

90 that runs alongside the border to Mexico.

Pumpville is about 8 or 10 miles off U.S. 90, built on the old Southern Pacific Railway tracks to replenish the old steam engines with water—thus its name, Pumpville. There is absolutely nothing left of Pumpville except a beautiful little brown stone church with a white, wooden outhouse. The town buildings are now just rubble, looking much like the immediate vicinity's brushy, hilly, terrain. Yet the church, originally Baptist, still remains active.

Members of the community church in Pumpville, Val Verde County, work during their annual clean-up day.

It just happened, on the day we were there, several families had gathered at the church to do some painting and cleaning up the grounds. It turns out they were getting the church ready for some missionaries that were due to live there on the church property.

With nothing else available as a gathering place, it was easy to see how this church had become the focal point of community life. Folks came from miles around to socialize, as well as worship. And by miles, we mean more than two or three.

One rancher we visited with said just to go to a grocery store in Langtry or Dryden was an 80-mile round-trip. Living out here, one had to make sure they remembered everything on their list, or it was a long way back to get that forgotten half-gallon of milk or loaf of bread. Makes you thankful for city life, if you're inclined to be forgetful.

Even so, the little church in Pumpville was just another example of how country churches have long been the meeting place that brought people together.

WE HEARD ABOUT a church in Atascosa County, a mesquite-and-brush covered prairie south of San Antonio, called The Old Rock Baptist Church, well over 100 years old, so we looked for it—not knowing where on earth it might be in this largely ranch country that ranks high in Texas for its beef production, as well as peanuts and watermelons.

We found it, near Somerset, on Farm-to-Market Road 3175 at FM 476, and sure enough, it was a church built out of red rock—not exactly native stone in these parts. There is a cemetery just to the right, and a historical marker out front, just two steps from the front door.

The Old Rock Church is an historic place. It was organized in 1857, in Somerset, just to the north in Bexar County, but later moved

The historic Old Rock Baptist Church, near Somerset, features huge red rock, constructed in 1867 by church members.

in 1867 to a 2.5-acre plot in Atascosa County where the church was built over a two-year period by local members. By the way, the church paid $10 for that 2 1/2 acres in 1867. The historical marker says that services began in Old Rock Baptist Church in 1869, dirt floor and all.

Unlike most churches of that era, this one was racially integrated from the very beginning, and the cemetery carries names of church members buried there, also reflecting many ethnic races. Also of note, the church was renovated in 1921 by a local oil company, and is today still a very active church.

From *Linda's notes*

Medina County — Medina County is full of historic small towns. One is Devine, which still boasts the working Shroud Blacksmith Shop, in continuous operation since 1903. It features hundreds of cattle brands burned on its doors. ... Devine has an opera house, and a nice bed-and-breakfast inn. ...Castroville is called "The Little Alsace of Texas," featuring German-style country cottages. The Landmark Inn first served stagecoach travelers, and still doesn't offer radio or TVs in its rooms.

We happened to find the state's—no, make that the world's—smallest Catholic church just outside of (where else but) Dime Box, Lee County, north of Giddings. Complete with a cemetery that virtually surrounds it, this little white steepled church is known as St. Martins Catholic Church. If you attend a service there, you'll sit on hand-made benches that can seat probably less than two dozen friendly faithful. It has a historical marker out front that claims this little church is the world's smallest Catholic church. I suspect there can't be very many churches of other faiths that are much smaller.

WE HAVE MENTIONED TIME and again how proud members of country churches are of their church, their community, their heritage, and their way of life.

St. Martins Catholic Church, just outside of Dime Box, Lee County, claims to be the world's smallest Catholic church. Its pews are hand-made benches.

From Linda's notes

Dimebox — I've always wondered how Old Dimebox, in Lee County, got its name. So that was my first question when we visited. One of the stories is seems it was originally known as Brown's Mill. Mail was picked up weekly and delivered to Giddings, the county seat. The carrier would then bring back mail and "other necessities" requested by residents of Brown's Mill, who would then leave a dime in the community box as a tip to the carrier. The Post Office eventually gave it the name of Dimebox since Brown's Mill sounded too much like Brownsville!
...Dimebox achieved national prominence in 1945 by being the first town in the U.S. to have 100 percent participation in President Franklin Roosevelt's March of Dimes campaign.

On our many trips around Texas, we must have passed through the tiny Kinney County town of Spofford three or four times. Located on Texas 131, just a few miles south of Brackettville—you know, where John Wayne's Alamo survived General Santa Anna and Hollywood's version of history—I can tell you there's not much to see in Spofford. Even the Southern Pacific freight trains that rumble through between El Paso and San Antonio don't stop here any more.

But Joe Cruz lives here, and every time we'd come through, we'd see Joe walking along the tracks or beside the highway with his herd of 10 or 12 goats. Joe always carried a stick, and a can full of loose corn kernels. When the goats would roam too far, he'd rattle that can of corn and they would hustle back to him. We never saw him "reward" his wayward wanderers, but I guess they all hoped that he would.

One day, we stopped to talk to Joe, and he asked if we had seen his church. We admitted that

Joe Cruz leads his herd of goats near Spofford, Kinney County. "You need to see our church," he told us.

44

we had not. There was really nothing within miles of Spofford but empty downtown buildings guarded by tumbleweeds, and a couple of dirt roads linking a few farms up with the highway. Joe replied: "You need to go see our church. My wife and I just finished painting it." He told us how to get to it—yep, down one of those dusty, dirt roads.

What we found was a quaint building, no name anywhere we could see, with a yard that was groomed, and a colorful flower bed that had been carefully maintained. Remember that Joe told us he and his wife had just painted the church? Linda described it as "electric blue"—meaning it was definitely different. But Joe was proud of that church, and ditto for the dozen or so parishioners who call that church home.

From Linda's notes

Kinney County — Not far from Spofford, on FM Road 1572, is the Texas A&M University Experimental Ranch. It has miles and miles of fence. I wonder if that is part of A&M's experimental research? ... Fort Clark in Brackettville, built in 1852, is now privately-owned and offers all kinds of facilities. It is a wonderful winter retreat, and you can rent rooms in the old Officers Quarters. ... Brackettville is an old historic town, very clean and interesting.

ANOTHER PROUD CHURCH member we met on our travels was Ben Simms, a member of the Methodist Church in Paint Rock, Concho County. Now this old church had, some years before, celebrated its 100th anniversary, in 1991—having been founded, of course, in 1891.

As Mr. Simms guided us on a tour of the old white, all-wooden church, we passed a commemorative baptismal font donated by Mr. Simms and his wife in memory of their daughter, who had been killed in an auto accident. The pride he had in his church, and of the gift, was just another example of the close attachment rural Texans have with their country churches.

IN THE FAR NORTHEASTERN section of Cooke County, near the end of FM Road 678 that leads into the Hagerman National Wildlife Refuge, on the south shores of Lake Texoma, there is a ghost town named

The Methodist Church in Paint Rock celebrated its 100ᵗʰ anniversary in 1991.

Dexter. I say ghost town. Perhaps 25 people live in the vicinity. In 1848, it was supposed to have been the county seat of Cooke County, except that the Butterfield Stage Line went through Gainesville instead. So now you know the rest of that story.

However, about the only structure left in Dexter today is a pretty white, non-denominational church, well over 100 years of age, which still holds Sunday services. In fact, there was a worship service in session when we arrived one Sunday morning, with about 10 or so

At the Dexter Community Church in Cooke County, we visited with John Brooks, part-time minister. Note the old pot belly stove.

cars parked alongside the road.

Not wishing to interrupt by coming in late, we drove past the little church, and the cemetery nearby, following the road that turned left to where the town used to be. We found an old bank safe back in the woods where the bank once was. Across the road were the remains of a hotel and saloon. (We later learned there used to be two hotels in the town of Dexter.) Also still standing was a building known as an Advertising Curtain Opera Hall—meaning they sold ads on the stage curtains to help pay for productions. The wooden benches of the opera hall were still there, though many had since collapsed, and the old stage still supported a piano. Linda said she could almost feel the excitement of a dressy Saturday night outing, standing there on the stage.

By the time we got back to the little church, services had ended and church-goers were coming out. We stopped and chatted with John Brooks, who turned out to be a part-time minister (in addition to his full-time job). He explained the history of the church while we toured the building. It hadn't changed much in 100 years. It was still heated by a pot belly stove. The sanctuary was one big room, but partitioned so that during Sunday School, the adults had one area, the school-aged kids another, and a kindergarten full of coloring books and crayons was located at the back of the church. For the big Sunday worship service, they would all merge into the center—no doubt close to the pot belly stove during the winter months.

From
Linda's notes

Concho County — Northeast of Paint Rock is the 1683 site of an early Spanish mission, Mother Maria de Agreda, established as a mission for Indians. Although Mother Maria never left Spain, the Indians could describe her in detail. "She came from the sky," they said. ... Paint Rock is also close to Lowake, home of the Lowake Steak House, the "biggest and best in Texas." Out in the middle of nowhere, it seats 140, and there's usually a waiting line. Great onion rings to go with great steaks!

WHEN YOU SPEAK of Texas country churches and crosses, you have to include the so-called "painted" churches of Texas. They might not be as small or quaint as most traditional country churches, but they are also found in the rural areas. They are so unusual, and are called "painted" churches because of the artwork painted on the inside, even though on the outside they might be as plain as most rural places of worship.

Most of the painted churches we found had some similar characteristics—generally featuring tall steeples that would rise majestically above manicured farmland—and usually sur-rounded by other buildings such as a school or rectory. Once inside, the artwork, the paintings, the statues are unbelievable. They are breath-taking.

Among the "painted" churches we visited included two in Karnes County, at Cestohowa and Pana Maria. At Pana Maria, a mosaic of a black

The Blessed Virgin Mary Catholic Church in Cestohowa, Karnes County, is one of many so-called "painted churches" in Texas.

Madonna is prominent, donated by a prominent Texas native: former President Lyndon B. Johnson. We also found four painted churches in Fayette County—Ammannsville, High Hill, Praha, and Dubina— communities of less than 100 people, probably only half that.

ONE COUNTRY CHURCH that was truly special was the Church of the Visitation, a rather large Catholic church in the little Falls County town of Westphalia, about 15 miles east of Temple (Bell County). Westphalia is not on the official map of Texas,

Mosaic of a black Madonna (above) at Pana Maria Catholic Church and the stained glass window at Blessed Virgin Mary Catholic Church (left) in Karnes County are typical art décor of "painted churches" in Texas.

but believe me, it's there, on Texas Hwy. 320, toward Marlin if you're traveling north.

This church was organized in 1882, with the present church sanctuary built in 1895. It is said to be the largest all-wooden church in the state of Texas. The original church building was destroyed by a storm, but rebuilt in seven months. Now that's a story of strong faith (and a lot of faithful volunteers, I bet!).

As I mentioned before, if you're interested in seeing Texas' many historic and unique country churches, remember they are located in places that don't

Church of the Visitation in Westphalia, Falls County, is the largest wooden church in Texas.

always show up on your official state map of Texas (and most won't). To see them—and other interesting venues off the beaten path—I recommend you invest in a copy of *The Roads of Texas*, your back road Bible if you want to know where you're going once you leave the I-20s and I-35s of this great state.✪

CROSSES— ON THE SUBJECT OF CHURCHES, I would be remiss

if we failed to mention two religious crosses that we came across that are musts if you are in the area. One is in Ballinger, in west-central Texas (Runnels County), and the other is in the Panhandle, an icon right on I-40 and Old Route 66 in Carson County.

When you drive into Ballinger, arriving via U.S. 83 from the north, and approach the courthouse square, you'll see a giant cross, over 100 feet tall. It first seems as if the cross is on the courthouse square itself, but it's actually several blocks away, off U.S. 83, in an open field. It's worth stopping for.

Known as "The Cross," it was erected in 1993 by Jim and Doris Studer as a thanks to the Good Lord for all the blessings He had bestowed on them. They had the cross built by Jansa Construction Company of Rowena, in the hope that those who view it may pause a moment to also thank God for their many blessings. It's indeed a blessed sight.

"The Cross" off U.S. 83 is a blessed sight in Ballinger, Runnels County.

But "The Cross" in Ballinger is a half-grown pup compared to "The Cross on the High Plains" at Groom in the Texas Panhandle. This colossal cross can be seen at least 20 miles before you get to it, situated some 30 miles east of Amarillo. That may speak as to how flat the Panhandle is, but it is also testimony to the size of this white-steel "statement." You can imagine how a giant cross structure, rising 190 feet (19 stories) into the Texas sky, easily dwarfs the semi-trucks that pass it on Interstate 40.

The Cross on the High Plains was designed and financed by Steve Thomas, president of Caprock Engineering, again to serve as one man's personal statement of faith. It's arm span is 110 feet, and the cross is estimated to weigh 1,250 tons. It was engineered to withstand 140 mph winds. At this writing, it still stands. ✪

"The Cross on the High Plains" towers 19 stories above I-40 at Groom, Carson County.

Scottsville Cemetery, near Marshall.

CHAPTER THREE

Cemeteries

I am not a cemetery connoisseur. Linda, however, would spot a cemetery on the detailed map we carried with us on our trips, and the next thing I knew, we'd be looking around and checking out grave markers. She would read the epitaphs on old tombstones and get quite emotional reading about a house full of six children dying from dysentery in just a short time, or finding the grave markers of children in their teens, killed in Indian attacks.

It's true that many of Texas' old cemeteries can tell gruesome tales—and that was just the way it was in the old days when our forefathers and other frontiersmen settled this great state hundreds of years ago. There is a lot of history and tragedy and sadness that can be found in our state's cemeteries. But humor?

Well, yes, in a way. While Linda would wander through a cemetery to look at old dates, or check out historically-significant events or persons, I would mosey along the grave markers to see if I could find more of the amusing or odd writings. I know it may sound crude to cruise through a cemetery to be entertained by inscriptions on a tombstone, but there are many interesting epitaphs that lend themselves to a guffaw or two. Looking for them might well get you into checking out cemeteries on your next trip off the beaten path.

Truthfully, there are many, many cemeteries in Texas that have been out there for years and years that are unkempt, with high growth hiding much of what you'd like to see, and some that are hard to get to. Others, of course, are extremely well-kept and—I hate to say this—even inviting.

The Youree Memorial Chapel at the Scottsville Cemetery near Marshall was built in 1904 and fashioned after a chapel in England. It is used for funerals and weddings.

One of the more outstanding cemeteries that is a must to see is in Scottsville, just east of Marshall (Harrison County), no more than 10 miles from the Louisiana border. When you're traveling east out of Marshall on old U.S. 80, go north on Farm-to-Market Road 2199 in

Scottsville, then turn right onto FM Road 1998. On the corner of that intersection is a large plantation house, sitting well back off the highway, surrounded by an iron fence. The Scottsville Cemetery joins the plantation property facing FM 1998.

The first thing you'll see is a 25-foot statue of a Confederate soldier, commemorating those who died during the Civil War. Just beyond the statue is a pond with ducks, and a beautiful gazebo that sits next to the water. The winding road past the pond and gazebo leads you to the cemetery itself. What you will see before you will take your breath away, for here are some of the largest, most elaborate—and no doubt, most expensive—gravestones you will ever see in any cemetery. The massive headstones surround a beautiful brownstone chapel, built in 1904, that sits back in a corner of the cemetery. The chapel was built by the parents of Will Youree, in his memory, after he died at the age of 31 of yellow fever. It is still used today, primarily for funerals and even weddings.

Under the plethora of pines and shady elm trees,

From
Linda's notes

Harrison County — You can't help but love the antebellum ambiance of this county! Marshall, the county seat, was also the "seat" of the Confederate government west of the Mississippi in 1861. ... The Ginocchio Hotel and old Texas & Pacific depot is absolutely beautiful. We just happened to be on hand for the grand opening of the restored depot, now a railroad museum. The courthouse, the cemeteries, everywhere you turn it's picture perfect! ... The Karnack Cafe in Karnack was a hotel and cafe built in the 1850s. Karnack is also the birthplace of Claudia Taylor, more famously known as former First Lady, Lady Bird Johnson. ... The Scott Plantation cemetery in Scottsville was ethereal. The Youree Memorial Chapel was fashioned after a chapel in England, all hand-carved interior with windows by Tiffany.

Above: Inside the Youree Chapel. Left: a Civil War moment at Scottsville Cemetery.

we found a lady artist with an easel, painting a watercolor of the chapel. It turns out that she and her husband lived on the plantation next to the Scottsville Cemetery as overseers of the grounds. Linda went inside with this lady to see the interior of the chapel, and reported how grand it was. The chapel is not open for public viewing,

Oakwood Cemetery in Huntsville (above) includes the gravesite of Texas hero Sam Houston (facing page).

so Linda felt our timing was, indeed, very special. When you take it all in—the pond, the gazebo, the giant gravestones, the chapel, the massive shade trees—this cemetery is such an inviting place to see and visit, and a must for anyone traveling in the Marshall area.

On par with Scottsville Cemetery is the Oakwood Cemetery in Huntsville, just off Interstate 45 in Walker County, about an hour's drive north of Houston. Now there are many nice reasons to visit Huntsville, other than to see a family member incarcerated in the state prison there (just kidding). It is one of the state's oldest cities, full of late 1890 and turn-of-the-century homes, the home of Sam Houston State University, a variety of art and antique boutiques and craft shops, a great eatery on the courthouse square—you name it, Huntsville is a place worth exploring. Ditto for Oakwood Cemetery.

Beautiful, well-maintained, sprawling under a forest of tall pine, the Oakwood Cemetery includes the gravesite of General Sam Houston, one of Texas' all-time famous heroes, having defeated the Mexican Army after the fall of the Alamo, allowing Texas to become

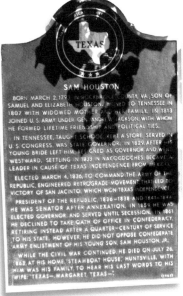

its own Republic, then being elected the Republic of Texas' first president. But there are other notable historical figures buried here, too, along with a preponderance of pioneers—many who were victims of the vicious yellow fever epidemic of 1867.

A section of the Oakwood Cemetery was set aside as the Negro section. This was the case in many graveyards of Texas—and no doubt throughout the South.

61

In the Negro section of Oakwood, as you might guess, there are many notable black pioneers buried. A lady by the name of Jane Ward, was a freed slave who for years ran a boarding house in Huntsville, where she also cared for sick folks.

Gravesite of Jane Ward, a freed slave, at Oakwood Cemetery.

Also buried there is Joshua Houston, the personal servant of Sam Houston.

AN ENTIRELY DIFFERENT setting for a cemetery in Texas is the Stiles Cemetery in the Stiles community of Reagan County, south of Midland. This is typical West Texas territory—flat plateaus, grass-covered prairie, and sandy draws that can quickly flood during a thunderstorm. The Stiles Cemetery is like a lot of Texas cemeteries: it's on private property.

Gravestone of Joshua Houston, servant of Gen. Sam Houston.

You can visit the cemetery by entering a private ranch off U.S. 67 near the county seat of Big Lake, then take a winding ranch road, about 12 to 14 miles, to get to the cemetery entrance. The Stiles Cemetery is rather large, and on a slight hill where the only building in sight is the now-deserted old county courthouse in Stiles (see the chapter on Old Courthouses).

When we went to the Stiles Cemetery, there were several crudely-prepared signs, on corrugated metal, stuck on posts, hand-written with white paint, along the ranch road that said: "Caution—Ewes Lambing." Now, you country folks know that means sheep were giving birth at that time of the year,

Linda joins County Judge Mike Wilkins at Stiles Cemetery. Upper right: hand-carved rock gravestone for longtime Reagan County rancher. Lower left: Grave marker for noted U.S. Cavalry horse buyer.

From Linda's notes

Huntsville — The city where Sam Houston lived, and is buried, is a wonderful place to visit. It is one of Texas' oldest cities, loaded with turn-of-the-century homes, and chock full of antique and arts-and-crafts shops. It is well mapped and marked for tourists. ... Historic buildings are everywhere, and museums too. Two include the Sam Houston Memorial Museum complex, on the 15 original acres belonging to General Sam Houston, including Houston's "Steamboat House"; and the Gibbs-Powell House Museum, built in 1862, and operated by the county historical society.

and you needed to be very cautious driving around that area. Despite the warnings, and our faithful eyeballing for ewes, we didn't see a single lamb. But what better place to give new life than in a cemetery, right?

There is a lot of history in the Stiles Cemetery if you just take the time to read the epitaphs. It was here that Linda mourned for those children who died in their early years due to one disease or another, along with those who were struck and killed by rattlesnakes—a fact of West Texas life that kept us on our toes while we toured the place.

Among the early pioneers buried here was John Patterson, who lived to be 91, and who bought and broke horses throughout West Texas and New Mexico for the U.S. Cavalry. We also found a huge rock, not the type normally found in a cemetery, obviously off a nearby ranch, in honor of John and Jo Ann Weatherby. John's date of death was noted, but there was no indication that his wife had passed on. The Weatherby name is well known as a ranching family in Reagan County.

A long-time sheriff of Reagan County is also buried here. The story goes that he and a friend had a serious argument in the hallway of the old courthouse in Stiles. The sheriff shot and killed his best friend, then walked into his office and shot and killed himself. The two "best of friends" are buried less than 100 yards apart.

BACK IN THE WILD COWBOY DAYS OF TEXAS, there were many gun fights just between good ol' boys who might have had a mite too much to drink, or truly "bad guys" who just wanted to pick a fight. Cemeteries are full of them. And many were buried with their boots on—some in the famous Boot Hill Cemetery in Old Tascosa in the Panhandle.

If you are traveling west from Amarillo on Interstate 40, then turn north on U.S. 385 toward Dalhart, you will come to the famous Cal Farley's Boys Ranch. It's in Oldham County and includes the ghost town of Old Tascosa on the Canadian River.

When you enter the 10,600-acre Boys Ranch, you'll pass by the Boys Ranch Zoo and past the old one-time courthouse of Oldham County (now the Julian Bivins Museum), and up a hill—maybe 500 yards from the entrance to the ranch—to Boot Hill Cemetery, no doubt named after the infamous Boot Hill Cemetery in Dodge City, Kansas.

This is a pretty rugged place, still maintained (though it still has that old-time ragged look), and full of shoot-out victims. Countless gun battles in places like Old Tascosa helped make the Old West so popular among pulp writers and B-movie makers—but Boot Hill really makes that part of Texas lore so real.

There are five gravesites in the Texas version of Boot Hill that

From
Linda's notes

Oldham County — Even though you think of the Texas Panhandle as being flat, the rugged, rolling terrain carved by the Canadian River makes this as picturesque as the Hill Country. ... The zoo at Cal Farley's Boys Ranch features animals brought in by locals and Park Rangers that were injured and nursed back to health. ... Adrian, on old U.S. 66, is an oasis in the northern edge of the South Plains. The Plains Fran House Cafe is not only a great place to stop for lunch, but you should check out the cute coop gift shop, full of beautiful hand-made articles, paintings, etc. ... The Hickory Inn Cafe in Vega has great stew and home-made pies.

Boot Hill Cemetery in Old Tascosa boasts five graves from one gunfight.

came from the same gun battle in Tascosa, on March 21, 1886. John Leverton, Jesse Sheets, Ed King, Frank Valley and Fred Chilton all died on the same night, in a gun battle started by a quarrel over Rocking Chair Emma, the local dance hall queen. According to local lore, Emma was severely wounded, and another fellow named Lem Woodruff (who shot and killed King, Valley and Chilton) was wounded twice, finally dragging himself three miles to a ranch house for help, using his smoking Winchester as a crutch. It finally took a Texas Ranger, Captain George Arrington, to end the bloodshed—killing Leverton, victim No. 5.

From
Linda's notes

Panola County — Panola is the Indian word for cotton, but it has more pine trees than cotton fields. ...
Carthage, the county seat, is a beautiful, historic residential town. ...
Carthage was not only the birthplace of country-western singer Jim Reeves, buried near here, but also the birthplace of Grand Ol' Opry icon Tex Ritter. ...
Aaron Provost says the Adams Store community used to be a slave farm. Slaves were paid with wooden chips that could be redeemed only at the Adams Store. ... The Lickskillet Store in the Bethany community now features antiques. ... The ABC Farm & Petting Zoo in De Berry is a great stop for children.

ON A TRIP TO CARTHAGE, Panola County in deep East Texas, I remarked to Linda that every time I would announce a rodeo in Carthage during my pseudo cowboy days, I would drive out east on U.S. 79, just a few miles out of town, to the grave of Jim Reeves, the popular country-western singer who was killed in an airplane crash in 1964, two weeks short of his forty-first birthday. I still feel "Gentleman Jim" Reeves was one of the great country-western voices of all time.

The story told about Jim Reeves is that he informed his family when his time came, he wanted

to be buried under oak trees near where the cattle grazed. When he died in the unfortunate plane crash, his wife was able to buy a plot of land right on the highway under some very huge oak trees.

Today, a barbed-wire fence circles the pasture where cattle graze, and where Jim Reeves is buried. There is a circle drive so you can pull off the highway, and a long, winding sidewalk that leads to the gravesite. As you walk toward the gravesite you will come to a giant guitar sculpture with a gold record inlayed in its center.

A statue of Jim, guitar by his side, overlooks the grave, and the inscription on the statue really tells a lot about the man. It reads:

"If I, a lowly singer, dried one tear,
or soothed one lonely, human
heart in pain,
then my only verse to God is
dear,
*and not one stanza has been
sung in vain.*"

A great verse for a great singer, a

Left: Walkway to Jim Reeves' gravesite near Carthage includes a guitar sculpture. Right: A statue of "Gentleman Jim."

great man, who died too young.

Incidentally, for many years, his widow brought fresh flowers to his gravesite every day. In the past few years, the State of Texas took over the maintenance of the grave site and keeps it beautifully maintained.

Jim Reeves' epitaph credits his Maker.

SOME CEMETERIES SHOULD BE VISITED just because of a quirk in history. Out in the Big Bend region of Texas, there is a little town (population 270) called Valentine, in Jeff Davis County, on U.S. 90 halfway between Marfa and Van Horn. I bet you've been there. It, too, has a cemetery, not very impressive, not anything other than maybe a conversation piece—because that was the cemetery that was featured in the epic movie, *Giant*. This classic film that starred James Dean, Rock Hudson and Elizabeth Taylor was shot in Marfa, but the non-descriptive cemetery in Valentine was picked for this one scene,

Valentine Cemetery in Jeff Davis County played a role in the classic film, Giant.

68

probably because it was so desolate.

EARLIER, I MENTIONED that Linda liked to peruse the headstones and check out some of the stories that the markers might tell about people who lived and died here.

There were many cemeteries that told of tragic events. These were hard for Linda, because very often the inscriptions on the grave stones showed how many young children died, either by disease, or by the hands of attacking Indians, in the early days of Texas. Our intent is not to demoralize the reader by mentioning morbid happenings, but there were

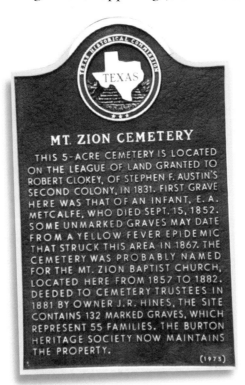

Mt. Zion Cemetery historical marker notes first grave was an infant.

From
Linda's notes
_____

Washington County — Brenham, the county seat, is a must visit. You could spend days exploring the town. ... "Must Be Heaven" is a great drug store. And check out the Ant Street Historical District. ... Blue Bell Dairy offers not only Texas' famed "Blue Bell" ice cream, but also a fun tour. ... Washington County is full of old plantations, especially in the William Penn community. Most notable is the John H. Seward Home, featuring hand-sawed cedar. ... The town of Independence was first called Cole's Settlement, settled by one of the original 300 families in Texas, and renamed in 1836 to commemorate Texas' independence from Mexico. ... Historical buildings are everywhere, including the Independence Baptist Church, third oldest Baptist Church in Texas, where Sam Houston was baptized in 1854. ... Chappel Hill reminds me of Salado, a tourist's dream town. The Stage Coach Inn, built in 1850, is now a bed-and-breakfast. Bevers Kitchen in an old house is also a must stop. And the old Chappel Hill College, started by the Methodist Church in 1852, is now a museum.

A "common grave" is noted in Proffitt, Young County.

two cemeteries we visited that should be noted.

In Washington County, at the Mount Zion Cemetery, we learned that the fourth burial in this cemetery was an infant, buried in 1852. There were also numerous unmarked graves throughout the cemetery, all victims of the 1867 yellow fever epidemic. Time and again, we noted that there were many deaths recorded in 1867 throughout the state from yellow fever.

In the Proffitt community, located in Young County, we found a "common" grave in the cemetery there which held three young boys who were slain in an Indian raid at Elm Creek in 1867, the same year of the yellow fever epidemic.

WHEN YOU VISIT as many cemeteries as we did, it's easy to run across tombstones of famous people—many you've read about in the history books.

Among the graves of well-known pioneers of Texas, we've already

Gravestone of Mirabeau B. Lamar, Texas' second president, dwarfs others in the Morton Cemetery near Richmond, Fort Bend County.

Grave of Elizabeth Crockett, wife of Texas hero Davy Crockett, is in Texas' smallest state park in Acton, Hood County.

mentioned that Gen. Sam Houston was buried at Oakwood Cemetery in Huntsville. Texas's second president (after Sam Houston), Mirabeau B. Lamar, is buried in the Morton Cemetery in Fort Bend County. In

Goliad County, we found the grave of Colonel J. W. Fannin, who led in the fight against Mexico and was killed at Goliad after the fall of the Alamo. And in Hood County, in the little town of Acton, near Granbury, we found the grave of Davy Crockett's second wife,

Gravestone at the Moffit Cemetery for J. Evetts Haley, author and rancher, and his wife Nita, came from the Haley Ranch.

Elizabeth. The cemetery is located in the Acton State Historical Park, Texas' smallest state park.

As we were touring Bell County in Central Texas, we went into the Moffat Cemetery and found a beautifully created red rock marker—probably came off the Haley Ranch—for J. Evetts Haley, well-known author, historian and rancher. The craftsmanship on the stone is worth the trip.

IN THE LITTLE FANNIN COUNTY TOWN of Leonard, we got involved in a discussion with an investigator from the Leonard Police

Lee Cemetery near Leonard is lost along a one-lane country road.

Department, and he asked if we would like to know about a really interesting, old cemetery. And he told us about the Lee Cemetery.

We found Lee Cemetery, thanks to his detailed instructions, for I doubt we would have on our own. There were no signs of any kind signifying this was a cemetery, which sits along a one-lane country road right on the Hunt and Fannin county lines. Before we even got there, I began to worry if I was going to meet another car, or how I was going to turn our Suburban around to head back. (As it turned out, we did have to drive another quarter of a mile past the cemetery before we found a turn-around.)

Lee Cemetery is surrounded by a chain-link fence and shade trees, not very-well maintained, with tombstones scattered here and there. But the one grave that stands out— and the reason it's called the Lee Cemetery—is the impressive gravestone of Captain Bob Lee, a Civil War veteran. Apparently, Capt. Lee was involved in a feud with some renegade Army deserters over old Civil War issues. He was shot and killed when he was ambushed in May, 1869, near the very spot where he is buried. Many other graves in the cemetery are also of Confederate veterans from the area. There was no indication, by the way, that Capt. Bob Lee was related to General Robert E. Lee, the Confederate

Confederate Capt. Bob Lee was buried at the spot where he was ambushed and killed by renegade Army deserters in 1869.

Army's famous leader.

Speaking of Confederate soldiers and cemeteries, we were surprised by a rugged, unkempt cemetery in Van Zandt County, north of the Midway community on Hwy. 64, off FM Road 314, called the Frontier Red Hill Cemetery. Many of the tombstones were damaged, and we don't know if it was because of vandalism

The Frontier Red Hill Cemetery in Van Zandt County (above) is historic, yet it appeared to have been ravaged by vandals (see below).

or just lack of care. Even so, there are some very well-maintained tombstones— and oddly enough, each one marks the grave of a Confederate soldier. This includes markers that  identified the Confederate soldier as "Unknown"—they didn't even have a name—but these were still carefully maintained.

Several Confederate vererans—including an unknown soldier—are buried in the Frontier Red Hill Cemetery in Van Zandt County. Two sisters who died two days apart in 1856 were the first to be buried here.

The road to the cemetery is bumpy, and it's one of those places that you can easily miss, but if you're ever in the area, and interested in old cemeteries with a bit of Confederate history, the Frontier Red Hill

Cemetery is a place worth the effort to see.

FAR OUT IN SOUTHWEST Texas in Kinney County is Brackettville,
halfway between Uvalde and Del Rio, on U.S. 90. There are many
interesting things to see here—not the least being "The Alamo"
movie set, which sits out on a high hill on Happy Shahan's ranch.
Here is where John Wayne, in 1959 as Davy Crockett, "fought" for
Texas independence. Some may even think this is the "real"
Alamo—all alone and mystique-like among the mesquite, far less
civilized than the truly historic Alamo in San Antonio, 100 miles
to the east.

There is also, on the south end of Brackettville, the old military
post, Fort Clark. Established in 1852, Fort Clark became one of the
most well-known military posts in the Southwest. It was deactivated
as a horse cavalry post in 1944, and today it's a private resort-
retirement community where you can buy condos or rent an
apartment and play 18 holes of golf for a week or weekend.

Near Fort Clark is a small cemetery that is most unusual. It is the
Seminole Indian Scout Cemetery, established for the descendants of
black slaves of Florida Seminole blood, who later settled here in the
1830s when they were pushed out West (most went to Oklahoma)

*Two of four Medal of Honor "buffalo soldiers" are buried side by side at the Seminole
Indian Scout Cemetery at Fort Clark near Brackettville, Kinney County.*

A U.S. flag marks the grave of a Medal of Honor Indian Scout at Fort Clark.

from the Southern plantations where they had lived. Many sons of those Seminole descendants became members of the U.S. Cavalry's legendary "Buffalo Soldiers" who helped protect citizens during the

Indian Wars of 1865-1876.

Trained as Indian scouts at Fort Clark, this particular regiment of black cavalrymen were named "Buffalo soldiers" by the Apache Indians because, historians say, the black soldier's hair resembled the buffalo's shaggy coat. The Buffalo soldiers were said to be respected by their Indian adversaries in the same way they respected the buffalo, which to the Apaches were deemed sacred. And by the way, four Buffalo soldiers buried at Fort Clark were awarded the Medal of Honor.

When you visit the cemetery, you begin to realize the great risks these soldiers had to endure—facing countless Apache attacks while on scouting missions, their post hundreds of miles from civilization, reachable only by horseback—but for the most part, they accepted their lonely, perilous life. Visiting here is a very humbling experience, a must visit along with John Wayne's replica of the Alamo, or the adjoining Alamo Village, a typical frontier town of the 1800s.

SOMETIMES, WE NEVER had a chance to visit a cemetery that we took the time to find. One such was the Gray Mule Cemetery south of Quitaque in Briscoe County, in Palo Duro Canyon country. Just the name intrigued us. The cemetery is in what once was called the Gray Mule community. It was getting dark by the time we drove out to it, and it had been quite a day of driving and visiting in the Palo Duro Canyon area, so we just never made it. Sorry, but one of these days, we will.

We were in Stonewall County, about an hour out of Abilene, heading to see the old county courthouse which is now a private ranch house on U.S. 380, just outside of Aspermonte. Near the old courthouse (now ranch house) is the Rayner Cemetery, located on the

From
Linda's notes

Stonewall County — The old courthouse in the Rayner community, built in 1890 at a cost of $40,000 and now a ranch house, was used as the model for the ranch house featured in the classic Hollywood saga, "Giant." ... The community of Old Glory was first settled by German immigrants and named Brandenburg. When World War I broke out, the American-German citizens petitioned the state to change the name to Old Glory, to show loyalty to their adopted country. ... The very modern high school in Aspermont is built underground, with the superintendent's office on the top floor.

The old Rayner Cemetery in Stonewall County was knee-deep grass and barbed-wire.

ranch road that goes past the ranch house. It's a bit of a rugged ride for 2.2 miles, and you'd better check for rattlesnakes if it's summertime, because this is rattler country.

The cemetery is fenced in, and a bit overgrown, and it looks like it

Like armed sentries, rows of cactus protect the old Randado Cemetery on a private ranch in Jim Hogg County.

Another "beyond the cactus" section of the old Randado Cemetery near Hebronville.

could be of some historical significance to the area—if only we had
the courage to climb the fence, hack through weeds, and hope we
didn't meet up with a rattler. Linda was sure she heard a rustle in the
grass (like a rattle?) and that just about took care of checking out
that cemetery. So if you go, let us know what you found!

In Jim Hogg County, south of Hebronville, on Texas Hwy. 16, we
came to a little ghost town of Randado. We almost gave up looking
for the town, because it is now enclosed within a working ranch,
including the little cemetery of Randado. We took some photographs,
but didn't stay long because we didn't seek permission (being on a
private ranch), but we could always say that "we've been there."

NOW, WHEN I GO INTO CEMETERIES, I'm more interested in some
of the unusual or odd epitaphs on the tombstones. A cemetery in
Falls County comes to mind. There was a gray stone marker, maybe
two feet wide and four feet high, and the message had been hand-
scratched, probably by a knife or maybe even a nail, with the writing

slightly slanted from left to right. The grave had the name of Clara Nichols, under which it read: "Died, 1921. Nov. 3." The November date appeared like it was an afterthought.

We found another similar marker in Fannin County. This one was a red sandstone marker, a stone probably hauled out of a pasture, and scratched in the stone by a knife were these loving words: "To Dad, With Love, Johnny." Crude, but touching.

In Gober, a community of 146, also in Fannin County, I happened upon a tombstone in which the message was very simple: "Aaron Hessenger—Age Unknown. Relatives Unknown. Killed in a Runaway Wagon." It leaves an interesting story for your imagination.

In Wood County, I found an unusual marker with a picture of a man on a horse that simply said "Killed by a Drunk Driver in Hopkins County." Now it appeared that the family of the deceased was slamming their neighbors over in Hopkins County, but who knows why they chose those last words for their beloved.

NORTH OF FORT WORTH, and west of Rhome in Wise County, we went into the Aurora Cemetery. I saw a tombstone that I thought was funny, but Linda didn't. She thought I was a bit male chauvinist, I guess. The tombstone was five feet tall, shaped like a tree trunk, and the inscription said: "Jim Chandler, and wife." No other message. No name for the wife. I thought that was odd, even funny. Linda still doesn't think it was that funny!

There is also something funny (or at least odd) that makes the Aurora Cemetery unusual. Local folks claim a space craft crashed in the Aurora area in 1897, and the pilot of that space ship is buried there. Now folks, we're talking 1897, not 1997. I understand that the cemetery folks have put up markers at the gravesite many times. And as soon as they do, somebody comes along and takes it as a souvenir. Couldn't be our friends from Mars (Van Zandt County), could it? Maybe Venus (Johnson County)? Even more far-fetched, how about

Saturn (Gonzales County)? There was no marker when we visited there. But they say it's a true story.

Also, in that same cemetery, there is an unusual message on a tombstone we did find. It's not a message that many parents would put on a tombstone of a two-year-old. But in the year 1893, Nellie Burns passed away at age 2. Her epitaph reads:"As I was so soon done, I don't know why I was begun." Sad thought, and hard to explain.

In Bailey's Prairie, a ranching community in Brasserie County, James "Brit" Bailey was buried in 1833, and folks around here claim that his ghost still roams the area. But what is unusual about his burial is that, at his request, he was buried standing up, looking west, his gun by his side. His reason: He did not want anyone looking down on him, even in death. No wonder they say his ghost haunts his onetime ranching empire!

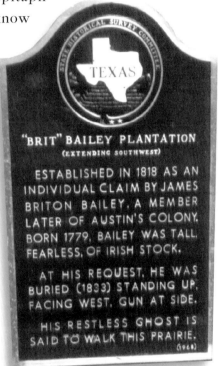

James "Brit" Bailey requested to be buried "standing up." Some say his ghost still haunts his onetime ranching empire.

When we were in East Texas, in Cherokee County just west of Ruse, we found a community full of Roaches. The community is known as Roachville, founded by T. J. Roach, a few miles beyond Maydelle on U.S. 84, and yes, it has its own cemetery. Everyone buried there are members of the Roach family. Now, at the back of the cemetery, a rather large tombstone marks the grave of the elder Mr. Roach, and buried with him are his five wives—Alice, Sally, Kate, Elizabeth and Josephine. According to the dates of death on each of the grave markers, Mr.

T. J. Roach is buried in the Roach Cemetery, along with his five wives.

Roach outlived three of his five wives.

Also in Cherokee County, near Linwood on Texas 21, there is a grave marker right at the entrance of a small cemetery for Helena Kimbell Dill Nelson. Buried in 1804, this lady was the mother of the first Anglo-American born in the state of Texas. Not only was this an historic gravesite, but it was surprising that we came across it.

A LOT OF HISTORIC cemeteries aren't right on a main highway. Some are really off the beaten path—more like an unbeaten path. Traveling north into Lamar County from Hopkins County on FM 2675, we turned right on County Road 24280. The reason we turned off on these county roads is because Linda had been told about this very historic cemetery and she wanted to check it out.

As you might guess, this was almost a non-road—two ruts that had been made by somebody who had driven this way a long time before. The grass, brush and weeds were pretty high on both sides of the Suburban, even scraping its undercarriage. Suddenly, we came to the end of that county road, without seeing any signs of a cemetery. And, of course, the terrain was such that there was no place for us to turn around. So we started backing up to get out of there.

Sure enough, after backing up well over a quarter of a mile, we spotted what appeared to be some tombstones maybe 50 to 75 yards off the rutted road. We got out, working our way through the briars and stickers, only to find the tombstones were not legible. We did manage, however, to read enough on three markers to realize this

From *Linda's notes*

Lamar County — Paris is so *magnifique, oui?* Ah, so is Paris, the county seat of Lamar County. The whole town is worth seeing, if no other reason than to absorb its beautiful Victorian architecture. But the show-stopper time is in mid-summer, when the crepe myrtle explodes with blooms that will take your breath away! ... The city holds its annual Crepe Myrtle Queen Coronation in July. ... Not far from the McGlassen Cemetery, between Enloe and Roxton, is Shelton's Fort, built for protection from Indian raids. Only a historical marker is left to see, though.

The historic but weathered McGlasson family cemetery markers in Lamar County were as hard to read as was the walk through briars and stickers to get there.

was the McGlasson family cemetery.

Rather than try to follow our off-road venture to the McGlasson cemetery, I would highly recommend that you check out the Evergreen Cemetery in Paris, county seat of Lamar County, where they are more than 40,000 graves—featuring many unusual, handsomely carved headstones and monuments of many early Texas patriots, dating from 1866. This large cemetery is on South Church Street at Jefferson Road.

ANOTHER CEMETERY that was an adventure for us was the Dunn's

Dunn's Fort Cemetery, on a Robertson County ranch, was not an easy find.

Fort Cemetery, located on a ranch east of Hearne, and just southwest of Wheelock, in Robertson County. Since Dunn's Fort is a designated state historical site, the ranch gates remain open for visitors who want to see the old cemetery—but it's not an easy find. We had to ask a rancher working on his fence how to get there, and he directed us to an adjoining ranch.

The entrance to the ranch property was basically a cattle guard sandwiched between two brick columns. From there, we drove a long way through a pasture to a second cattle guard, and into another pasture. Feeling like we were on the verge of being lost, we spotted a small ranch house and headed in that direction—watching a coyote

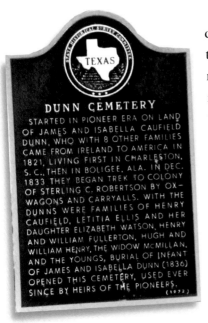

Burial of two infants started this family cemetery in 1836.

dash out of our way—just as we saw the marker to Dunn's Fort. Yep, the marker was next to a fence near the ranch house. The fort was created in the 1830s by a rancher named James Dunn as a place of safety for area families due to constant Indian attacks. He picked his property as the site of the fort because it was the highest point for miles.

While I was reading the historical marker, I noticed that a lady was sitting on a chair in the doorway of the old ranch house. She finally rose from her chair and yelled: "Hell, come on in. I'm not going to bite you!" And so we did.

While she made tea, we had an enjoyable visit with Adrienne Pryor. She lived alone, her husband having passed on just two years before, so she knew the history of the ranch well. We told her that our purpose for driving there in the first place was to see the cemetery, and she was kind enough to lead us to it. It was back in a brushy, wooded area—and even though it was fenced, it would have been hard to find.

Her husband's grave has the only modern-era gravestone; most of the other grave markers told of those killed during the Indian raids. And off to one side, there were more than 50 little white crosses, with no names. She said those were slaves who were killed during such raids—buried in the same cemetery as were the other pioneers.

THERE WERE SEVERAL cemeteries that brought home the strife that early settlers faced during Texas' bloody era of war-like battles

From
Linda's notes

Trickham — The community of Trickham, in Coleman County, got its name for all the jokes played on people at the general store. ... Trickham is the oldest town in the county. ... It is rumored that John Wilkes Booth, assassin of President Abraham Lincoln, taught school here. ... All three churches in Trickham—the Baptist, Methodist and Presbyterian—meet in one building, called the Union Church.

between pioneers seeking to settle, and hostile Apache and Comanche wild game hunters who sought to restrict the western movement of whites into their hunting grounds.

On a ranch near Abilene, in Taylor County, we found an unnamed cemetery about a hundred yards off the road, behind a barbed wire fence. I was not particularly in a hurry to walk through rattlesnake country to see what was there. We were told later, by an area resident, that everyone buried in that cemetery was killed by Indians. In Coleman County, in the ghost town of Trickham, there are graves above ground, with one marker that reads: "These unknown pioneers gave their lives in the winning of the frontier. Their names are known only to God."

In Limestone County, northwest of Groesbeck, sits the reconstructed military post known as Fort Parker. It was built in 1833

In the Trickham Cemetery, several graves are above ground.

A unique grave marker in Trickham for unknown pioneers of Coleman County.

by three Parker brothers to protect the nearby settlement of eight or nine homesteads. In 1836, the fort was overrun by several hundred Comanche, killing five and taking five more captive. One of the captives was Cynthia Ann Parker, then 9, who grew up with the Comanche, even married a tribal chief, and later became the mother of the last great Comanche chief, Quanah Parker.

A large monument on the old Fort Parker site overlooks the graves of many victims of Comanche and Kiowa (Apache) raids that terrorized this area for years. The cemetery is known as Fort Parker Memorial Cemetery.

Near the ghost town of Fry, in Brown County, we discovered the Mud Creek Cemetery, its graves full of settlers killed in Indian attacks. And in Hamilton County, there is a community called Indian Gap, sporting a building that once served as its post office, grocery store and saloon. High on a nearby rugged hill is a 20-foot monument dedicated to the early settlers of the area. It is totally surrounded by graves, many victims of Indian raids that terrified settlers throughout this part of Texas.

Impressive monument at old Fort Parker honors those killed in Indian attacks.

IT'S NOT SURPRISING that old country cemeteries are the final resting place for many of Texas' early settlers—simply because they settled in the rural environs of our state, enduring the tough times when Texas was still a big part of the Westward Movement.

While we concentrated on old country cemeteries while traveling the back roads, we did check out a few cemeteries in our great cities, too—like the State Cemetery in Austin. Unofficially known as the

Above: The Mud Creek Cemetery in Brown County is full of settlers killed by Indian raids. Below: Monument to settlers at Indian Gap, Hamilton County.

"Arlington of Texas," the State Cemetery's monuments mark the resting places of 2,000 patriots, statesmen and heroes of Texas, including the tomb of Stephen F. Austin.

For the most part, however, Texas history—and the interesting characters and brave pioneers who shaped our state in its early years—tended to live out their lives and passed on in the vast wind-swept plains of West Texas, or the giant timber country of East Texas, or the rich blacklands of North Texas, or on the flat, fertile, sandy grasslands of South Texas.

The backroads of Texas are literally dotted with the markers of men and women whose epitaphs tell an interesting story about our state. It was a great experience, and an adventure in history that we will always cherish. ✪

Pondering a move on the Sabine County courthouse lawn in Hemphill.

CHAPTER FOUR

Domino Games

So you think baseball is America's pastime? I assure you there's a lot of old gentlemen in the State of Texas who probably love and follow baseball, but their No. 1 pastime is playing dominoes.

As we traveled around the state, checking out many small towns, it wasn't uncommon to see a little old building, probably 10-foot-by-10, maybe 12-by-12, somewhere near the downtown area, with a sign that designated it as the Domino Hall or Domino Parlor. Often times, the sign depicted only a simulated domino piece with white dots on it—no fancy words like "Domino Parlor," because everyone knew what it was.

These unobtrusive places, often squeezed between more upstanding places of business, were usually closed, because it was "open" only when the guys in the "club" or "association" would gather to play their favorite pastime game. Some would play in the mornings only, some in the afternoons, and some would make it an all-day affair.

It was a great experience for us to happen in on some live domino games. Often, I wished I had a video camera to capture the scene. But then, these old guys would have probably thought they were movie stars and they would have had us talk to their agents and pay big money to film them.

Domino players are an unusual group of people. Those who are busy playing around the table will not look up, much less talk

From
Linda's notes

Scurry County — Snyder, the county seat of Scurry County, was founded by a buffalo hunter, Wm. H. (Pete) Snyder, who built a trading post on Deep Creek. ...A white buffalo statue on the courthouse lawn commemorates J. Wright Mooar, who killed 20,000 buffalo including white buffalo. ...Snyder was named one of 11 All-American Cities in 1968. ...Fluvanna once had a 30-room hotel, when it had a population of 500. ...There is a "dugout" in Camp Springs. Also, Indian remains and prehistoric petrified wood have been found in the area.

to you. Those standing around, like vultures sitting on a fence, waiting to dive in when someone loses, are a bit more sociable. They'll visit with you a little bit.

SOMETIMES, DOMINO PLAYING is the only thing going on in town. In Fluvanna, located in the northwest corner of Scurry County, we found very little left in the downtown area that would indicate there was anything going on. But then, we spotted two older gentlemen coming out of a small little building, which looked like an old Post Office (and once was) but now sported a fading anti-litter sign that said *"Don't Mess With Texas."*

As was our custom, we stopped, introduced ourselves, and they in turn told us their names— one was Joe Landrum and the other Guy Turner. Joe told us they were leaving the daily domino

Talking to Joe Landrum and Guy Turner, outside the domino hall in Fluvanna.

game in Fluvanna that had just ended, locking up the building that once served as the old Post Office, then became a barber shop, and now was the town's domain for domino games.

Curious about the rules of etiquette when it comes to playing dominoes, I asked Joe: "When you gather to play, who gets to play the first game?" Joe thought about it, then replied matter-of-factly, "The first ones there." Usually there's four who start, and when the first two lose, there's two more to take their place. "If you're lucky, you can play all day," said Guy. "But I reckon we've got some serious players, so there's usually a pretty good rotation."

WE DID HAPPEN onto a domino game at Grapeland, in Houston County, in an old, old general merchandise store that had turned itself into a junk emporium. I mean, this was not just used merchandise. It was used and reused and used again stuff, and you could hardly walk into the place it was so jammed. Over in a crowded corner, a domino game was going on.

There were four players, and maybe five or six observing, supervising or waiting to jump in. One of the on-lookers happened to be the editor of the local newspaper. We visited for a while, talking low so that we didn't interfere with the more serious matters at hand, then he asked if we were going to be around for a bit. He said he wanted to run back to the newspaper office, get his camera, and take a photograph of us with the domino players. We agreed, and he returned and took a photo. Some weeks later, we got a copy of the photo that appeared in the *Grapeland Messenger*

From
Linda's notes

Houston County — Darsey's Grocery & Hardware store in Grapeland began business in 1886, and the present store was built in 1913. It's a fascinating place, and so were owners George Darsey and daughter Catherine. ...County seat is Crockett, named for Alamo hero and frontiersman Davy Crockett. Marker at Crockett Springs says Davy stopped here to camp on his way to the Alamo. ...Crockett has beautiful old homes. A tour of them is a must! ...Kenny Rogers is from Crockett and probably had his records played at the local radio station, KIVY. .. The beautiful Methodist church in Crockett was built in 1901 of bricks fired at the site. ...In Austonio, the Texaco station will mail letters for you. There is no official post office in town. ...The little red schoolhouse in Ratcliff was started for freed slaves.

Hangers-on await their turn in Grapeland

newspaper, along with a story about us and our travels.

When we visited Bastrop, nestled in the piney woods of Bastrop County, we went into an antique mall—Linda is a big lover of those

kind of places—and we moseyed all the way into what turned out to be a feed store. And there, in a well-kept corner of the store, we found a game of dominoes going on. There were two tables, eight folks involved in the game, and perhaps another eight eagerly waiting their turn. I talked to a lanky on-looker, a rancher with a big silver belt buckle and western hat, who had just left

In Bastrop, "it just goes on and on, all day, until they lock this place up."

as a participant at one of the tables. He said the games had been going on most of the day. "It just goes on and on, all day, until they lock this place up, I reckon," he said in his slow South Texas twang.

ON THE DAY WE visited Pickton, just past Como out of Sulphur Springs in Hopkins County, we found a small country grocery store. It was about noon time, so we stopped to get a little something for lunch. Just across the street, there was a crowd looking into this little place where I figured right quick there was a game going on. I watched for a little while from our car, then stepped out with my camera which had a zoom lens and walked across the street to take a photograph of the players through the door. I noticed that a couple of them looked up. They probably thought we were the IRS or FBI. I then put the camera away in the car, and we went into the grocery store.

As in most small towns, there was a small grill at the back of this grocery store, so we ordered some hamburgers. In a few minutes, this gentleman wearing overalls came over to where we were. He didn't introduce himself to us, but very to-the-point said: "Those domino players across the street

From
Linda's notes

Pickton — How little towns pick their name is always fascinating. That includes Pickton, northeast of Sulphur Springs in Hopkins County. It was settled in 1856, but didn't amount to much until the old Red River Railroad decided to build a station on its east line. A committee was formed to name the station. They had trouble picking a name, so they decided to call it Pick Town. The railroad changed it to Pickton. ...Country store owned by Jack Brown has a grill in back. Good hamburgers and home-made pies! ...A scene from the movie, "Crysalis," was shot inside the general store.

In Pickton, they got leary of camera folks with telephoto lenses.

Domino halls are easy to find—they stand alone, and lean a little. These are in Pickton (above) and Como (left) in Hopkins County.

wanted me to find out who you people are." We naturally introduced ourselves to him. "Tell the guys we're okay," I told the ombudsman in overalls, "and when we finish our burgers we'll come across and say hello." And we did. We found four players who never looked up—one surprisingly in his 20s, most of them in their 60s or older.

Naturally, I got into a conversation with a couple of guys on the sidelines. I was born in Hopkins County, and I was relating to him about my childhood times out in the Martin Springs community. How

Serious domino players never look up.

the subject of World War II came up I'll never know. But it did, and I mentioned about the day shortly after World War II started when I rode in the wagon with my grandparents from the farm all the way into Sulphur Springs, which was seven miles, but felt more like 70. We made that wagon trip so my Uncle Ben, the youngest son of my grandparents, could answer his call to duty, having been drafted into the United States Navy.

I was telling this story, but before I could finish, one man standing alongside who already knew what my last name was, blurted out "That wasn't Ben Jennings, was it?" As soon as I said it was, he drawled "Well, I took that same bus when I was drafted." That was just one of my Small-World-Small-Town experiences traveling the backroads of Texas.

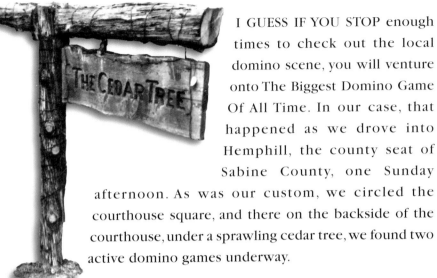

I GUESS IF YOU STOP enough times to check out the local domino scene, you will venture onto The Biggest Domino Game Of All Time. In our case, that happened as we drove into Hemphill, the county seat of Sabine County, one Sunday afternoon. As was our custom, we circled the courthouse square, and there on the backside of the courthouse, under a sprawling cedar tree, we found two active domino games underway.

Under the cedar tree, on the Sabine courthouse lawn, The Game goes on and on.

DOMINO GAMES

Once again, there were four players at each table, and this time maybe a dozen or more spectators watching the games from benches. Nearby was an attractive hand-carved sign, nailed to two cedar posts, that said simply "The Cedar Tree."

We spent most of our time visitin' with the friendly folks who were watching or waiting their turn, but the players once again never looked up. Their eyes were fixed on the domino pieces laid out in front of them. I don't think any of the eight players ever batted an eye. If lightning had struck, I don't even think they would have looked up for fear they would lose a turn or miss a point.

I suspect if we went through Hemphill today, and stopped to see The Only Game In Town Under

Sabine County — In the Sabine National Forest, we encountered what the locals call "love bugs." They were so thick we had to wash our vehicle several times a day. ...In Geneva, there's a historical marker for a Spanish rancho called El Lobanillo, built in 1773, said to be the oldest continuously-occupied site in East Texas. ...An old drug store in Hemphill had a toy train running through. ...Ben Smith has bought many old buildings in town and is restoring them. ...McMahans Chapel near Hemphill is the oldest Methodist church with continuous service in Texas, going back to 1833.

The Cedar Tree, it would be the same two games we saw on our trip some years ago. It could well be true that the old cedar tree on the courthouse lawn in Hemphill was just a stringy sprout of a twig when that game started eons ago. I don't think The Cedar Tree is listed on any historical society's tree logs, but maybe it should be.

And I reckon The Biggest Domino Game of All Time is still going on—one of many that can be found in virtually every small town across our big state of Texas. ✪

The Domino Club in Spur, Dickens County.

In Throckmorton, guess which door is the domino parlor.

Some domino halls don't need fancy words. This one is in Perrin, Jack County.

In Ben Arnold, you don't need much room for tables, chairs and serious players.

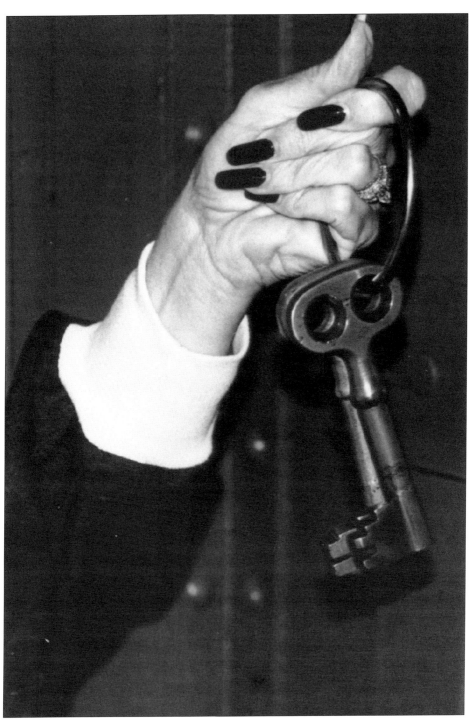

Keys to the old jail in Stanton, Martin County.

CHAPTER FIVE

Jails and Cell Blocks

Old jails—and their cell block cousins—are an integral part of Texas lore. Not that they still are used as *hoosegows* or *slammers*, for there are many old jails that are now refined as city offices, libraries, museums and other such niceties.

Linda and I even found one old county jail in Vernon, county seat of Wilbarger County, that is now an antique store. It still displays the old cells complete with iron bar doors along with every thing else

Not all jails are still jails. This one, in Vernon, is home to Jailhouse Antiques.

you can imagine. But the old cell doors weren't for sale.

We found many old county jails in Texas were built alike. They normally were two-story buildings, built of native stone, and usually separate from the county courthouse. In the old days, the sheriff and his family lived on the first floor, and the prisoners were housed on the second floor.

NOT MANY OF THESE old county jails are still operating today as jails *and* residences, but we found one that was. It was in Crowell, county seat of Foard County in West Central Texas, and home to about 1,200 law-abidin' people, give or take one or two.

When we drove into Crowell one sunny afternoon, we found several people out on the lawn of the old jail, no doubt trading tales and gossip and enjoying a nice day. Among them was the county sheriff.

James Jennings trades jailhouse stories with Foard County Sheriff Bobby Bond.

Now when you travel Texas, and you see a county sheriff, you know he's the sheriff without asking. They all look alike. I told Linda "There's the sheriff and I'm going to meet him." She didn't ask how I knew. The hat, the gun, the cigar—it all fits the image.

Sheriff Bobby Bond and I had a nice visit, and when I asked if he lived there, he said he didn't, but that his top deputy and the deputy's family lived there. And true to tradition, they lived on the first floor, and the jail itself was on the second floor. But that wasn't all that was in that old jail house.

THE DEPUTY'S WIFE was the dispatcher for Foard County, and she also operated a one-chair beauty salon in the back room on the first floor of the jail house. It was the only beauty salon in town that I know of. That's what I call catering to a "captive" audience.

Anyway, Sheriff Bond asked if we wanted to go up to see the jail itself. Having been a Dallas police officer for many years, I wasn't particularly interested in seeing another jail cell. But Linda was, because she was curious about how the jail worked and how the doors interlocked and so on. So we went up one flight of stairs to the jail level, where we saw two men in orange coveralls in the open area, just milling around.

When the sheriff reached the second-floor landing, he announced "Alright, boys, back in the cells. We've got company." The two guys in orange coveralls walked around the corner, opened their cell doors, and walked inside. They even locked the door behind them. I didn't see any sign that said I would be fined talking with prisoners, so I chatted with them while Linda learned all about interlocks and such from Sheriff Bond.

It just goes to show it's a different world out beyond the Interstate highways where men trust men, and a handshake is more common than a shakedown.

But beware talking with prisoners elsewhere.

Mum's the word at the Hockley County Jail in Levelland.

Out in the flat West Texas high plains of Hockley County, we stopped by to check out the county jail in Levelland and drove around to the backside of the building. There was a sign painted on the wall above the rear door with a heavily barred window. The sign simply proclaimed: "$10 fine to talk with prisoners." I didn't inquire what precipitated that sign, but I was glad I wasn't under the same rules back in Crowell.

And speaking of prisoners, while passing through another small West Texas town on a Sunday afternoon, we saw prisoners on a vacant lot across from the jail just sunning and relaxing and having a great time. Folks in town told us they do that every Sunday. They say there's no danger of any prisoner "taking off" because, first of all, he's wearing bright orange coveralls, and secondly, "there's no place to go."

From
Linda's notes

Hockley County — The Spade Ranch just outside of Levelland was started in 1889 by Isaac Ellwood, who invented the barbed wire. His descendants still own and operate the 128,000-acre spread. ...Levelland is appropriately named for its flat terrain. ...There are several colorful mosaics around town, including on the chamber of commerce building, the hospital and the college campus. ...The school in Pep, in the northwest corner of the county, is now an alternative school for dropouts.

The old jail in Gonzales has a great museum.

The Gonzales Jail Museum features a "hanging gallows."

In the Gonzales Jail Museum, the door is always open to visitors.

ANOTHER OLD JAIL we enjoyed is in Gonzales. It has a great museum, and the hanging gallows are still there. Spring is a good time to visit Gonzales, as well as just down the road to Cuero, because this area has some of the finest wildflower fields anywhere in Texas.

OVER IN THE CAP ROCK country of West Texas, we visited Gail, the county seat of Borden County, and the only town in Borden County. It's a town of about 300 population, where the high school doesn't have a football field, but they do have a rodeo arena, and—get this—the town had a new jail.

We met R. D. Lewis, who was the sheriff at the time, and he told us that this new jail was two years old before it got its first prisoner. In fact, things are

From
Linda's notes

Borden County — Gail, the county seat, is the only town in Borden County. ...Both the county and the county seat were named for Gail Borden, a surveyor, editor and trustee of the Texas Baptist Education Society that founded Baylor University. He also invented condensed milk and founded Borden Foods ...We visited with Rich Anderson, who owns the Muleshoe Ranch. ...Borden County may be the only county that doesn't have a railroad going through it. It also doesn't have a bank, theater or hotel.

In Gail, it's so peaceful the old Borden County jail is no longer in use.

so peaceful out there in Borden County that the Highway Patrol doesn't even have a full-time patrol unit assigned, and the sheriff's department doesn't include traffic control as part of their job. "Nobody's ever complained about speedin' around here," he said.

That naturally got my attention, but what was even more startling, I also learned that there hadn't been a death in Borden County for almost three years.

Could this be the place we all wished to find in our lifetime? Could this be better than Utopia, Texas, one of the great, great places to visit and stay and live forever? I was naturally curious about the fact you don't ever die in Gail, but I learned the facts from a rancher named Rich Anderson. I asked him "What's the secret to life here?" and he answered: "Sir, it's pretty simple. We don't have a doctor in Borden County, we don't even have a hospital here, and if you're gonna die, you have to go to either Big Spring or to Snyder."

ONE LITTLE JAIL that also comes to mind is in Lipscomb, the county seat of Lipscomb County, about as far as you can go in the northeast corner of the Panhandle. Now Lipscomb is a beautiful place, not incorporated as a town, there are no paved streets, and it seems to be home to more wild turkeys than people. But we did find two parked cars at the sheriff's office, and no other activity going on in town, so we went in.

From Linda's notes

Lipscomb County — The county seat, Lipscomb, looks like something out of a Thanksgiving storybook. Turkey seem to roam the streets of Lipscomb freely.

Sandy Atkinson was on duty as the dispatcher for Lipscomb County. She's also the jailer. She also cooks for the prisoners. In addition, she does the prisoners' laundry; and she's in charge of the prisoners' exercise program. Still, she took the time to visit and

In Lipscomb, there are 33 residents "and not one of them is in jail."

The Lipscomb County Sheriff's Office enjoys a slow Sunday afternoon.

make us feel welcome.

We asked Sandy about the town of Lipscomb, since it was not incorporated, and looked more like a movie set than a real town. She replied:"When everyone is at home at one time, I think we may have 33 people in town. And by the way, not a single one of them is in jail."

NO CHAPTER ON JAILS would be complete without mentioning cell blocks. Now a cell block is very crude, but sturdy, built so that it could never be destroyed. These cell blocks were built so they could hold a prisoner until the county sheriff could come and transport them to the county jail.

They can be constructed in all shapes and sizes, but usually they are rather small buildings—not exactly designed for comfort or to watch TV—probably no larger than 10-foot-by-10, maybe 12-by-12. Some are one cell in size, some divided into two holding cells. We saw several that are worth mentioning.

One cell block we found was in Spofford, Kinney County, about 12 miles south of Brackettville. This cell block was out in a field where the grass and weeds have grown waist high, and this one was a two-cell dandy. It was about five foot wide and 10-foot long, made of metal strips woven together like a basket. That meant there was nothing to

This cell block in Spofford is not a place you'd want to stay very long.

stop anything like the wind or cold. There was no water nearby, certainly no "facilities," if you know what I mean—no bathroom or electricity—and certainly a place you would not want to stay very long.

There were two metal bunks, one per cell, and an eye-full of graffiti on the bunks and on the floor, and—since there were no walls—on the inside of the woven metal strips. A briar patch would be more pleasing than that old cell block in Spofford.

ODELL IS A LITTLE PLACE near Vernon in Wilbarger County, almost into Oklahoma, and while there we visited a local grocery store that didn't have a lot of groceries, but it had an abundance of photographs on the wall of people who lived there, or had lived there. Linda got

From
Linda's notes

Wilbarger County — Vernon, the county seat, is the headquarters of the famous W. T. Waggoner Ranch. ...The population of Vernon, according to its city limit sign, was 12,001. I wonder how many people thought they were the "one." ...The old jail is now an antique store called "The Jailhouse Village." Police cars still park there. Guess old habits are hard to forget. ...The city was named by the Post Office after Mount Vernon, George Washington's home on the Potomac. It wasn't the town's first choice. The town was originally named "Eagle Flat." ...Billie Adams runs his sister's store in Odell, Cooper's Grocery, which is plastered with pictures of folks who live in Odell.

Right: A cell block sits in the middle of a plowed field near Odell. Lower right: Inside, a rusty iron bed.

into a conversation with a neat lady who was running the store, learned a lot about the town, then we left. But only about two or so blocks away, we noticed this crude structure, off the road, in a plowed field.

I told Linda that it looked like a cell block. We stopped the car and walked into the plowed field. Indeed, it was an old cell block that had not been used in a long, long time. It was made of concrete, the door was gone, and there was nothing inside except an old iron bed. The one thing that caught my eye was the plowed field. The farmer who obviously tilled the land just went around this structure, and left it to the winds and the whims of nature. It was obviously not going anywhere. Such is the nature of cell blocks.

PASSING THROUGH GLAZIER, population 48, just outside of Canadian, in Hemphill County, we saw a cell block about two miles

out of town. It sits no more than five feet off the pavement of the highway, and perhaps you've seen it if you've ever been out that way. It's a 12-by-12 foot stucco building with bars on the windows and door.

I went into town and found a gentleman, Ed Howard, who was plowing his garden on a little tractor. I figured he would know why that cell block was sitting out there on the highway, two miles out of town. When I asked why, Mr. Howard smiled, puffed a

This cell block near Glazier didn't move an inch when a tornado hit in 1947.

little on his pipe, and drawled, "Well, let me tell ya. Several years ago, some cowboys came into town and one of them got really drunk. So they locked him up in that cell block. His friends decided they were gonna break him out before daybreak, so they lassoed that cell block and that's as far as they could drag it."

Well, when a good ol' Texan says, "Well, let me tell ya," you're about to hear a "windy"—you know, don't let the facts get in the way of a good story. Well, Mr. Howard had his fun, then he got down to the truth: "The original town of Glazier was destroyed by a tornado some years back," he said, "and they just rebuilt the town two miles further down the highway. The cell block has stayed put ever since." ✪

From
Linda's notes

Hemphill County — Canadian, the county seat, is known as "The Oasis of the Panhandle." Ironically, it's located on the Santa Fe Railroad line, and not on the Canadian River itself. ...The old Buffalo Wallow Battlefield, fought in 1874, is southeast of Canadian, and was one of several along the Canadian River that marked the end of Indian hostilities in Texas. ...The Palace Theater in Canadian has been restored, and has an 80-year history.

Timing to see some of Texas' off-the-main-road museums is critical.

CHAPTER SIX

Museums
Off Main Street

*M*useums *of Texas*. Now, there's a title of a table-top book for you. So go out and do your work! But a word of warning: Give yourself plenty of time, take reams of paper or note pads, cases of film, extra batteries for your camera—we could go on and on.

Indeed, there are many, many museums in Texas and each has a theme, a cause or a "calling." And each plays an important role in showcasing Texas and Texana. And yet almost forgotten are those out-of-the-way rural enclaves of local and area history, and some that are

The Texas State Aquarium in Corpus Christi — very impressive, very big, and a must see.

just, well ... well, read on.

Not included in this writing, by the way, are Texas' most popular and well-known museums—like the Texas State Aquarium in Corpus Christi, which is very impressive, very big, and a must if you are in the area.

In our travels to every town in Texas, there was really no way we could visit every museum. We just didn't have the time. Okay, we didn't take the time. If we did, and if we were able to check out each and every museum in this state, I think we'd still be on the road, probably in some small town waiting for the museum to open.

FOR A LOT OF MUSEUMS we came across and wanted to visit, Linda and I were there on the wrong day, or the wrong time on the right day—because some don't open but on one day of the week, or for just a few hours, say on a Thursday and Sunday.

From
Linda's notes

San Patricio County — There is a monument in San Patricio commemorating San Patricio de Hibernia, patron saint for whom two Irishmen, McMullen and McGloin, named their Irish colony in 1828. ...The old San Patricio Cemetery has markers for men who died defending Texas. ...Sinton, the county seat, is home to the Welder Wildlife Refuge, largest privately-owned wildlife refuge in the world. The Welder Ranch was established from a Spanish land grant more than 150 years ago.

Take the Blackland Museum in Taft, a town of 3,300 in San Patricio County, virtually on the Texas Gulf Coast. We went to visit the only museum in town and found it closed. An old wood sign, emblazed with writing from a wood-burning kit, explained why it was closed: "Thursday 10-12, 1-4. Sunday 2-5." In other words, you're limited when you want to tour the Blackland Museum in Taft. We just got there on the wrong day.

It was *déja vu* all over again in Sierra Blanca, Hudspeth County, right on Interstate 10 in far West Texas. We had just visited the unique white stucco courthouse in Sierra Blanca and, upon leaving the parking area, we spotted an old railroad depot and a deteriorating hotel that faced the tracks. The hotel obviously hadn't been used in years. The depot itself was well-cared for, nicely painted, and there was a

In San Patricio, the Blackland Museum is limited to two days for visiting.

Intriguing as the Hudspeth County Museum may be, it's only open on Wednesday afternoon.

From
Linda's notes

Hudspeth County — The mercantile store at Fort Hancock was started in 1883, now run by the Farris family. It has old fixtures and a historical marker inside. ...The cafe/gift shop in Cornudas, on U.S. 180, was a stage stop in 1856. The cafe has table legs that look like cowboy legs—complete with jeans and boots. The jeans and boots were donated by Wal-Mart truck drivers, they say. ...Just off I-10 are the ghost towns of Esperanza and McNary. Some old buildings are still standing.

big sign out front that read: "Railroad Depot. Hudspeth County Museum. Southern Pacific and Texas Pacific met here 1881." So we figured right off that it was a historical place.

Naturally, we parked the Suburban and got out to visit the museum, figuring it had a lot of railroad memorabilia and area artifacts, and would be enjoyable to browse around. I figure it must have been a Thursday or Friday. Maybe it was Saturday. Nonetheless, when we walked up to the door, there were two more signs. One was a commercially-printed one that simply read: "Closed." To the right of the door was a smaller, home-made sign that read: "Hours Wed. 1-5."

So if you want to visit what appears to be an interesting old railroad museum in Sierra Blanca, plan ahead and come on a Wednesday, after lunch.

AS WE TRAVELED the state for days and weeks at a time, our trusty backroads map of Texas was not marked with X's showing where all the museums are located. We zigged and zagged through towns and counties, and so many of the museums we found we came across by

Automobilia Village near Rosanky, Bastrop County, pictured above and below, is a unique museum that you would never expect to see on the back roads of Texas.

chance, and in places we would never expect to find a museum.

The day we were traveling down Texas 304 in Bastrop County is an example. We were in ranch country, nearing the little town of Rosanky, and about 300 to 400 yards to our left, off the highway, was a large ranch house and barn. There was a sign on the front of the barn, which we couldn't read from the road, but the very large iron arch gate leading to the ranch house was an easy read: "Automobilia Village, Central Texas Museum of Automotive History." As it turned out, the museum—in the beautifully-maintained barn— was closed, and so it was another "find" that will need to be visited later. But this was the case in so many off-the-main-road places that we just happened to drive by.

From
Linda's notes

Bastrop County — In the little community of McDade, it was exciting to come upon a movie in the making, "True Women," a CBS movie starring Dana Delany. People were walking around in period dress. And the movie sets around town were unbelievable. ...The Bastrop State Park features the "Lost Pines of Texas," a stand of pines 80 miles from the main pine forests of Texas. ...A historical marker about Josiah Wilbarger, who lived 20 years after a Comanche scalping, claims he credits the ghost of his sister for directing rescuers to him. She died in St. Louis the day before the scalping. ...Smithville, like Bastrop, is another walking treasure. Beautiful homes and a great old historic downtown make up the National Register Historic District.

WHILE DRIVING in Hardin County, in the Big Thicket piney woods of southeast Texas, which is oil country as well as a mecca for lumber mills, we drove into the little community of Batson, population 140, and stopped to take a photograph of a rather old Masonic Lodge. Just across the street, there was a gentleman unloading some drilling equipment from the back of his pick-up truck. He was dressed in some rather oily, greasy overalls that told me he had just come back from working on an oil rig—or else had been standing under one that had hit pay-dirt. Naturally, we got into a conversation.

He answered some questions I had about the old Masonic Lodge. He had lived in this area all his life, like many we met who have never left the place of their birth. Then he asked me: "Did you folks happen to see the museum downtown?"

James talks with Bates Hobbs about the Oil Patch Museum in Batson, Hardin County.

Now, I must admit that I didn't know Batson *had* a downtown. All I remembered seeing when we drove through was a service station/garage on one side of the road that goes through Batson (Texas 105), and a grocery store across the street. Well, that *is* the downtown of Batson. And we learned that the grocery store was once a grocery or general merchandise store, but is now the Oil Patch Museum, which had only recently been opened by the local town folk.

Naturally, our friend was very proud of their town's one and only museum, small as it was, and unopened as it was on the day we came through. In fact, there were no signs indicating what days, or what times, it *was* open. As our friend told us, it was still relatively new and obviously staffed by local folks when they were available to open its doors. But if you happen to drive through Batson, check out the

A one-of-a-kind museum in oil patch country—namely Batson, Hardin County.

Oil Patch Museum. It has to be a one-of-a-kind museum in oil patch country.

ANOTHER TINY MUSEUM we found—no bigger than the Oil Patch Museum in Batson—was the La Paz Museum in San Ygnacio, Zapata County, along the Rio Grande about 50 miles south of Laredo. It was a nicely-kept up stucco house, no bigger than two rooms, which could easily date back to the mid-1700's when this part of the country was first settled. The only sign on the building was hand-painted, on a wood cut-out resembling the state of Texas, with the name La Paz Museum, but no indication of the hours or days of operation.

The La Paz Museum is in a building that dates back to the mid-1700's.

As it turns out, we learned that the La Paz Historical Museum is a typical Mexican home circa 1790's, and includes photos of yesteryear Zapata, antique ranch furniture, 18th century cooking utensils, and early doctor's equipment. To see the museum, contact the elementary school in San Ygnacio. But the museum is open only when the school is in session, September through May.

AS WE TRAVELED TEXAS, we noticed that the population of a town or village has nothing to do with whether it has a museum. Take Bigfoot, in Frio County. It's not a big town by any stretch of the imagination. It doesn't even have its population posted on the village limits sign. Some sources say there are about 75 residents living in the area.

From
Linda's notes

Zapata County — When we arrived in Zapata, high school students were decorating a float for the home-coming parade. Zapata is the home of Falcon Lake, which divides Texas and Mexico. ...San Ygnacio looks like Old Mexico, with ancient stone houses. Love the band shell in the center of town. ...Uribe Street has old rock buildings, some restored beautifully. ...At the Farm & Ranch Supply in Falcon, they sell "hog traps."

The little log cabin in Frio County where Bigfoot Wallace once lived is now a museum, "open by appointment."

Bigfoot got its name from an early-day Texas Ranger, William A. (Bigfoot) Wallace, a well-known, well-liked lawman who resided here when he was doing good things as a Texas Ranger, Indian fighter and fighter for Texas independence. The community had been known informally as Connally's Store until 1883 when locals came up with Bigfoot as the official name for its new Post Office.

The little log cabin where Bigfoot Wallace once lived is now the Bigfoot Wallace Museum. It was another museum that was closed, and we couldn't get inside to see it. We later learned that it is open by appointment only, and you will need to "inquire locally." This could be a challenge, since there is no chamber of commerce or visitors center in Bigfoot. But there is a Bigfoot Church in Bigfoot, and a huge oak tree that splits the middle of a highway as you come into town, where you might be able to hail down a local citizen and ask about the Bigfoot Wallace Museum.

Also in Bigfoot, by the way, near the Bigfoot log cabin/museum, is another log cabin, two stories high, with double wooden front doors, two shuttered windows above the door, and steps on the left-side of the building that lead to a side entrance. It looks like what might have been an old hotel, but it's not, because the sign on the front says "This building is a replica of the one in Washington-on-the-Brazos (Washington County) where the Texas Declaration of Independence was signed." There is nothing that says it is a museum, too, and no mention of hours that you could visit. It may be part of the Bigfoot Wallace Museum, or maybe not—but again, we were not able to check it out.

From
Linda's notes

Frio County — Pearsall, the county seat, claims to harvest 55 million pounds of peanuts per year. No wonder they have a statue of "the world's largest peanut." ...The Old Frio County oil Museum showcases early Frio County settlers and Indian artifacts. Open Saturday and Sunday only.

OFF THE MAIN STREET of Flatonia, population 1,346, in Fayette County, we found a replica of an old jail, and across the street an old two-story building with an historical marker. It had at one time been

If you're a Roy Rogers fan, there's a little private museum in Flatonia worth visiting.

Roy Rogers mementos are perfect for those who believe good guys wear white hats.

the city hospital, and later an opera house. Just to the side of the main doors that once led into the hospital/opera house, there was a glass door that was open, leading into what appeared to be a small general store. So we went in.

Well, it wasn't a store. It was a museum, of sorts.

What we found was a two-room display of photos, posters, and western paraphernalia—all featuring my boyhood heroes Roy Rogers (along with Dale Evans) and the Lone Ranger! Now this was my kind of store! Except, there was nothing for sale. It was all part of a private collection, and the owners just choose to share it with those who happen by.

The collection included everything from cars to lunch kits to BB guns. There was even a bunk bed with a Roy Rogers bedspread, and Trigger lamps on each side of the bed. Now, as a kid who grew up believing white hats belonged to the good guys and black hats were worn only by bad hombres, this little "find" truly made my day even though, as museums go, it probably wouldn't make the Fortune 500 of Museums.

ROSSTON IS ONE of those Texas towns that is just this side of "Resume Speed." It is on a wide place in the road, officially marked Farm-to-Market Road 922, in Cooke County. It's halfway between Era and Prairie Point. The first thing we saw in Rosston when we drove into town was an old, tin-roof plank-board grocery store, a rustic porch across the front facing two hitching posts, three old gas pumps and an ice storage box. We noticed it because it was plastered with old metal signs advertising everything from Star Fertilizer to Kelly Tires to Nutrina Feeds—every weathered sign a collector's dream.

Painted in white, the old store's hours were posted: "Open 7, Closed 6. Xcept Sunday." As I recall, this was a Sunday. So we didn't go in with our grocery list.

Across the road, however, was an unpaved parking area where an

The unique Pastime Museum in Rosston, Cooke County (right photo), has no doors, but is a favorite gathering place for locals, located across the street from the Rosston General Store (above) and includes old tractors and other farming and woodworking equipment.

old tractor sat under a huge shade tree. The tractor looked like it had been retired some time ago. And just off a bit to the left, there was an old building that caught my eye. The back and one side of the building was enclosed, but the front and a part of the other side of the structure was totally open to rain, wind and curious people.

Approaching this curious building, I noticed there was some very expensive-looking wood-working equipment and containers of tools. Then I noticed the sign. It was made of wood, and read: "Pastime Museum."

This odd little place could well qualify as the most unusual "museum" in Texas. It is the focal point of community life. Old-timers gather, just like they might at a Dairy Queen in Quanah, and talk politics or solve world problems while they "work" with their woodworking machines. It's not a museum in the sense that it's open for tours or tourists. But then again, there's no front door, and no front wall, so it's literally "open" every day, day and night, and it's called the Pastime Museum.

MOST MUSEUMS CHARGE admission, and there's an obvious reason for that. Some do not, and that's rare. One of those rare museums that didn't—and was a surprise find to boot—was in the little community of Turkey, Hall County, in the rolling hills just south of the Prairie Dog Town Fork of the Red River. Now if you've never been to Turkey, it's because you didn't get off the main road—the main road in this case being U.S. 287 between Childress and Memphis.

From
Linda's notes

Turkey — We loved staying in the Turkey Hotel in Turkey, Hall County, when Jane and Scott Johnson owned it. Went back several times to keep in touch with their ventures. They made the hotel "a home away from home," decorated in the 30's and 40's decor. ...By the way, there are no door locks. We happened in one afternoon at 2:30 p.m., went through front door, didn't see anyone, but heard voices in back yard. Everyone was having tea, silver service and all. ...Jane made a recipe for sweet potato pancake mix which is marketed throughout Texas. Delicious!

Turkey is the home of the 1927-Flapper era Turkey Hotel, and it is also the birthplace of Bob Wills, the King of Western Swing, who was reared on a farm just north of here. And in Turkey, they have the Bob Wills Museum.

Now, you'd think that a museum as important as the Bob Wills Museum, in a little town named Turkey, wouldn't be hard to find. We asked about it, and were told it was located in the City Hall, which turned out to be a former school house. We walked in and found a nice, elderly lady at a counter.

When we asked if this was where the museum was, she said "Yes, it's the first door on the left, right down the hall. Would you like to see it?" We told her we would, and I asked if she sold tickets to see the museum.

"Oh, no," she said, shaking her head. "We don't charge anybody to see the museum. Just a minute, and I'll get a key and take you down

Turkey is the hometown of Bob Wills, and the little-known Bob Wills Museum.

there." When she returned with the key, we followed her to a door, then went inside. "Just stay as long as you wish," she smiled, "but let me know when you are finished, so I can lock it back up."

The Bob Wills Museum proved to be quite a place. Memorabilia of the Texas Playboys and of Bob Wills' career is neatly displayed in two rooms. There were some of his famous fiddles, boots, hats, old "78 rpm" recordings, and many, many photographs. As I was looking at some of the photos of his tours and travels, I spotted two ladies I had known since the 1950's, Teddy and Betty Lamb, well-known trick riding sisters who performed in rodeos around the country. They were pictured leading a western-theme parade in downtown Dallas. Yes, the Bob Wills Museum would have been worth an admission, but it was free to whomever wants to see it. Just ask for the key, instead of a ticket.

DRIVING BETWEEN Paint Rock and Eola, in Concho County, we came upon a sign on a ranch fence post that said it was the Barrow Ranch, and then it mentioned "museum hours." It was hard to believe we were anywhere close to where a museum might be. Curiosity got the best of us, so we entered through the ranch gate and followed a dirt road that passed a herd of longhorns grazing in the pasture, eventually reaching what appeared to be a working ranch headquarters.

There were four very large metal buildings and, as it turned out, this was the Barrow Ranch Museum. And what a museum! It was so fascinating that we spent hours looking—hours that we didn't think we had time for when curiosity took us by the hand and led us down that road. But it was worth the time we didn't have.

Each building, separated into sections, housed some 40 years of collecting—from early farm and ranch equipment to around-the-world collections. There was a section on early-American dining rooms, complete with an old pump organ. There was a "War Room," with a lot of World War II memorabilia, including captured German and Japanese flags. Another section was a large display of old washing machines, radios, record players and even vintage Victrola players.

There was the largest collection I've ever seen of Indian arrowheads, perhaps 15,000 in all, and other archeological artifacts. There were collections of china and glass cats, Oriental carvings and furniture, gems and minerals.

The Barrows Ranch in Concho County is where you'll find longhorns and four barns full of around-the-world collections.

An early-American dining room collection includes an old pump organ at the Barrows Ranch.

And we just happened on to this rare display of museum memorabilia, out where the wind blows. It seemed to reflect the Indian meaning of the county's name, Concho—"good returns from blowing wind." A visit to the Barrow Ranch Museum was indeed a good return on our investment in time.

The Barrow Ranch Museum is located about 4 ½ miles east of Eola, on FM 765, and is open Thursday through Saturday from 10 a.m. to 5 p.m., and on Sunday afternoons. And there is no admission.

MOST SMALL MUSEUMS focus on the history of their town or area. And often as not, a town's history is linked solely to the railroad that came through town—or actually caused the town to be born in the first place.

The Railway Express Museum in the Roberts County seat of Miami, population 540, is such a place. Miami originated as a railway construction camp on the Southern Kansas (later Panhandle & Santa

The Railway Express Museum in Miami, Roberts County, is located in the old restored railroad depot.

Fe) Railway in 1887. The Railway Express Museum (now known as the Roberts County Museum) is, of course, located in the old, restored railroad depot, and focuses not only on its rail camp beginnings but also on the cattle ranching industry that once provided 90 percent of the county's agricultural income.

By the way, if you just happen to mosey into Miami the first weekend of June, you may hear some pretty awesome high-pitched hollerin'. Miami holds the National Cow Calling Contest every year in the city park, and they've been doing that since 1949. Now don't ask me what they do with the cows that come a-calling during the contest!

MUSEUMS AREN'T ALL historical in nature. There are museums, big and small, that are theme-oriented. They focus on a slice of Texana— from air power to wind power.

We were having a good country breakfast in Huntsville at a little cafe across the street from the Walker County courthouse and noticed, nearby, the Texas Prison Museum. Huntsville, of course, is home to

The Texas Prison Museum in Huntsville is a better way to "see" prison life than living it.

the state's largest prison and headquarters of the Texas Prison System. Now if you're into this sort of thing, this museum is a far better way to see the ins and outs of prison life than being incarcerated as a convict.

141

The bus station in Huntsville is where many inmates go to find their new life—hopefully a better life—after they are released from the state's prison system.

As mentioned in a previous chapter, I spent a good many years as a police officer in Dallas, and I usually don't go out of my way to visit jails or prisons. But this little museum is fascinating. From ball-and-chains used in the old days, to "Old Sparky," the electric chair used from 1924 to 1964, exhibits tell the story of the Texas prison system. There are a variety of weapons—from rifles used by Bonnie and Clyde to illegal guns made by inmates inside the walls of the prison itself.

As with most museums we visited, this one is highly recommended, and it's not that far off Interstate 45. The Texas Prison Museum is located on the south side of the courthouse square. Ironically, it is just a few blocks from the rather busy bus station in downtown Huntsville where many inmates go to find their new life—hopefully a better life—when they are released from prison.

SPEAKING OF THEME museums, one of two that will whet your appetite is the Dr Pepper Museum in Waco, McLennan County. It's also not too far off the Interstate (I-35), and the museum is in

The original Dr Pepper Bottling Company plant in Waco is now the Dr Pepper Museum.

the restored, nationally-historic 1906 building that served as the headquarters for Dr Pepper Bottling Company before it moved to Dallas in 1923.

The unique Texas-invented drink goes back to the 1880's when a young pharmacist at Morrison's Old Corner Drug Store in Waco began work on a medicinal concoction that was tasty. It became a popular "health" drink at the drug store, then known as a "Waco." Then a beverage chemist named Lazenby further tested the mixture, named the drink Dr Pepper, and his formula is still in use today.

At the museum, we learned why the Dr Pepper logo features a clock showing 10, 2 and 4—those were the times of the day that research in the early 1900's showed people experienced an energy "let-down." Therefore, Dr Pepper became known as the "pepper-upper" drink.

We also learned that the Texas drink was first introduced at the

1904 World's Fair in St. Louis, the same exposition in which the hamburger, the hot dog, and the ice cream cone were also introduced to the world. So Dr Pepper arrived in good company!

By the way, there is another unique thing about Dr Pepper—since the 1950's, they dropped the period after Dr, which I guess means its name is now as odd as its fizzy medicinal flavor.

But it's not the only Dr Pepper museum in Texas. In Dublin, 70 miles southwest of Fort Worth, in Erath County, the old Dr Pepper Bottling Company plant is still operating, and they are still filling the old-fashion six-ounce returnable bottles on the old-fashion bottling line that you can see from the street.

The Dublin facility was the first franchised plant to bottle Dr Pepper, beginning in 1891, and it still uses pure cane sugar instead of artificial sweeteners. Obviously, it gets a lot of visitors. It features you-know-what memorabilia. The Dr Pepper Bottling Museum is open Monday through Friday, but the actual bottling is done on Tuesdays only.

IF YOU'RE NOT IN A HURRY, and most of the time we weren't, then coming into a town like Columbus, the county seat of Colorado County, when there is a parade going on is an added bonus. This was the town's annual Springtime Festival, and there was everything from bands to floats to FFA displays on the back of pick-up trucks and flat-bed trailers. Even four and five-year-old girls dressed in their frilly outfits were riding tricycles, tooting the horns mounted on their handle bars. This is something, of course, that you naturally stop for, and we thoroughly enjoyed a respite from road travel.

Over on a corner, near the courthouse, I happened to notice a rather strange-looking structure with a historical marker. Now, Columbus is a town full of historical markers, but this one really caught my eye. It was a round, stone tower that seemed to be

An 1883 stone water tower in Columbus is now a Confederate Memorial Museum.

four stories tall. It was shaped like a turret of a castle with an arched doorway and a narrow front slit of a window above the door. Folks had brought their lawn chairs to view the parade from the front of this historic castle-like tower. But as the festivities ended, those watching the parade began to take their lawn chairs and head for home, so we walked over to see what this place was all about.

What we were looking at from across the street, and wondering about, was an old stone water tower. Constructed in 1883, its 32-inch thick walls involved the laying of 400,000 stone bricks. It is now the Old Water Tower and United Daughters of the Confederacy Museum. Because it is a historic town, where the early settlers of Texas established their first colonies, Columbus—now a town of 3,916—has at least four other museums. Yet, for pure intrigue and interesting motif, the Old Water Tower in downtown Columbus is well worth a stop and a photograph.

From
Linda's notes

Reeves County — Town of Toyah has many photo opportunities, thanks to some magnificent ruins. I explored the gym built in 1912, now abandoned, but home of 5,000 rattlesnakes! Or so we were told. ...Fred and Sharon Sanchez were building an old mock town as a tourist attraction. ...Pecos, the county seat, is known for being the home of the first rodeo, and also for the Pecos Cantaloupes, the delight of gourmets throughout the U.S. thanks to its alkali soil, sunlight and altitude (plus irrigation). Harvest time is usually late summer.

PECOS IS ONE of my favorite cowboy towns in Texas. That's because it was the birth place of the Old West sport that caught on like a wild bronco, the rodeo. Once a hangout for rowdy cowhands and trail drivers, the town held a cowboy ropin' and ridin' contest in 1883, thus giving it the distinction of being the "Home of the World's First Rodeo." And the town of Pecos, in Reeves County, still holds its annual West of the Pecos Rodeo every Fourth of July.

It is also home to a true Texas cultural icon— the rustic West-of-the-Pecos Museum, which is located in the historic Orient Hotel that was once the finest anywhere in the West, or at least West of the Pecos River.

The West-of-the-Pecos Museum is located in the historic Orient Hotel in Pecos.

An old horse-drawn water wagon is among western artifacts at the West-of-the-Pecos Museum.

The museum and old hotel is located at the north end of the downtown area, just beyond the old red-brick Texas & Pacific Depot. You can't miss it. There is an old caboose that sits right in the middle of First Street.

There is a slight charge to go into the museum, but it's for a good cause. The museum underwent a $600,000 renovation in 1995, and the museum exists solely through donations and admission.

When we entered the museum, we found ourselves in the old lobby area of the Orient Hotel, full of ornate fixtures and accurate displays of life from the mid-1880's to the early 1900's. The museum has 50 rooms of exhibits, showcasing the law and lawlessness of Texas beyond the Pecos River. Visitors really enjoy the long mahogany bar in the museum's old saloon area where a mannequin dressed like a saloon keeper stands ready to serve your favorite sarsaparilla.

The old saloon itself has quite a history. In 1896, the year it opened, its quick-draw bartender, Barney Riggs, out-drew two outlaws, shot and killed them right on the barroom floor. Bronze markers and a bullet hole show where the gunfight took place.

While the museum's displays inside are very fascinating and worth the admission, outside the hotel-turned museum there is a replica of the Jersey Lilly Saloon, where Judge Roy Bean was said to have served his own brand of justice that became known as "the law west of the Pecos."

Next to the replica of the Jersey Lilly, guarded by rock pillars and a wrought-iron fence, is the grave of Clay Allison, known in the 1880's as "the Gentleman Gunfighter." As I recall, Clay Allison was the gunfighter who was reported to have said "I never killed a man that didn't need killing." He died in 1887—the day before the Fourth of July—but not by gunfire. He was crushed to death by his own wagon.

The grave of "gentleman gunfighter" Clay Allison is in Pecos. He died not from a bullet, but from being crushed to death by his own wagon.

SPEAKING OF JUDGE ROY BEAN, he actually practiced his "law west of the Pecos" in Langtry, Val Verde County, off U.S. 90, about 50 miles west of Del Rio. Langtry now boasts a population of 145, and there is a Travel Center and rest stop operated by the State of Texas, where bus loads of travelers stretch their legs, obtain official state maps and brochures from around Texas, and get a cool drink of water. And just off the little courtyard of the visitor's center is another replica of the Jersey Lilly Saloon.

Judge Roy Bean's court rulings at the Jersey Lilly Saloon were known as "the law west of the Pecos."

Compared to the restored Jersey Lilly in Pecos, this one looks like the "before" in a "before and after" advertisement. It is very plain and very weathered, and in so many ways it's even more realistic inside than the one in Pecos. Being there, you felt like the old judge might walk in at any moment.

By the way, Roy Bean's title of "judge" may have been a bit juiced up by ol' Roy himself. Some historians say he was really just a justice of the peace, and others wonder if that was even the case. But he did

Judge Roy Bean was a showman, so why shouldn't the opera house in Langtry be named after him? This building was also once the official "Town Hall and Seat of Justice."

administer justice in his own way, uncontested.

Just two blocks down the street from the Visitors Center and Judge Roy Bean's Jersey Lilly, you can walk to the banks of the Rio Grande, facing Mexico. And with a little effort, you can actually throw a rock from Langtry to Mexico. It's no wonder, out here in no where, why Judge Roy Bean was so liked, and so respected.

IF YOU THINK LANGTRY is out by itself, you should visit Stillwell Crossing. It's in Brewster County, out there in Big Bend country, and it has a population of three. But it's for real, and it is the home of the Old 4-L Ranch, and what is left of the old Stillwell

From
Linda's notes

Val Verde County — The old Southern Pacific Railroad had a pump station and cattle-branding operation at Pumpville until the 1950's. ...The county name means "green valley" in Spanish, but most of the green is sage brush. ...Bob Hinds, who was painting the Baptist Church in Pumpville, said they average one cow per 100 acres.

Hallie's Hall of Fame Museum south of Marathon honors Hallie Stillwell, the straight-shooting ranch matriarch who lived just short of her 100th birthday.

ranch house.

A well-marked ranch road (FM 2627) off U.S. 385, about 30 miles south of Marathon, led us to the little Stillwell RV Park and Store. Nearby is an adobe ranch house, the home of the Hallie Stillwell Hall of Fame Museum, honoring the witty and hard-working woman who ran the 33,000-acre Stillwell cattle ranch for 79 years.

We had the pleasure of touring the museum with Hallie Stillwell herself, and her daughter, Dadie Stillwell Potter, who managed the museum. Hallie was then about 97 years young, and was one of the most hospitable ranch matriarchs we've ever had the honor of meeting. (Sadly, Hallie Stillwell passed on a few years later—two months and two days short of her 100th birthday.)

The building that houses the museum is made of adobe brick, crafted from mud and straw collected a few yards across the road. It is as large as a meeting room and includes memorabilia she collected while living the life of a Texas ranch woman. It also includes a replica

The original one-room Stillwell Ranch house is part of Hallie's Hall of Fame Museum.

of the one-room shack that was the original ranch house in 1914. The unique family museum was dedicated on Hallie's 93rd birthday in 1990.

Museum artifacts include rustic ranch furnishings, the same wood stove that Hallie and Roy Stillwell used to cook meals for themselves, their two sons and ranch hands, a set of three-pronged forks dating back to 1871, and a cast-iron kettle that Hallie said "I hoped I would never see the likes of again!"

Thanks to our visit to Stillwell Crossing, and the Hallie Stillwell Hall of Fame Museum, we learned a lot about the rugged ranch life in early-day Texas, and especially the role women—this woman, for sure—played in taming this rough and remote land called Big Bend country.

SHAMROCK, IN WHEELER COUNTY, is an emerald along Historic U.S. Route 66 in the Texas Panhandle—and here on the flat plains, it's

The Pioneer West Museum in Shamrock is housed in what was once a "drummers hotel."

about as different from the mountains that ring Stillwell Crossing in Big Bend Country as mid-day is to midnight. As you travel east on Interstate 40, you could miss the Shamrock turnoff and end up in Oklahoma. But you don't want to miss Shamrock, else bad luck may befall ya.

Aye, laddie, if you want a bit of good luck, you might find it in Shamrock. A chunk of stone from Blarney Castle in County Cork, Ireland, is embedded in a crude concrete monument that is regularly painted green. And just in case folks don't happen to stop and find Elmore Park, where the Blarney Stone is on display, there is another more attractive (but less authentic) "Blarney Stone," closer to the highway, and embossed with a loveable leprechaun and instructions to kiss the stone "for everlasting good luck." A horseshoe embedded in the base apparently acts as a Texas good luck charm as well.

Perhaps the real "emerald" of Shamrock is not a stone, but a

A formal "tea room" parlor is one of several bygone era room settings at the Pioneer West Museum.

museum—the Pioneer West Museum. It's housed in the old two-story Reynolds Hotel, a so-called "drummers hotel" that catered to salesmen in the 1920's and 30's. The museum has 20 rooms of fascinating exhibits, focusing primarily on regional history. There are displays on early-day police and vintage weapons, Plains Indian culture, farm and ranch artifacts, and room settings that include an old upright piano in a formal "tea room" parlor.

Naturally, there was an emphasis on the city's Old Route 66 days when traveling cross-country by car was really an adventure. Back in the 1930's and 40's, Old Route 66 was the main road—the "Mother Road"—that crossed Mid-America, from Chicago to California. It passed through the Panhandle of Texas, offering travelers stop-over

Those who serve as postmaster are revered in places like Shamrock.

places like Shamrock.

Even today, not far from the Pioneer West Museum itself, you can see evidence of the old Route 66 days, such as the architecturally-artistic U-Drop Inn gas-cafe-motel stop in Shamrock, that helped create a Hollywood aura to early-day car travel and adventure.

Suffice to say, you have to get off the interstate to see museums that give a unique slice of life in Texas.

WHEN PEOPLE in the Dallas area ask "Where can we go and see Texas for maybe a day or a night?"—and sometimes a day trip is all the time folks have—Linda and I recommend they go east on old U.S. Hwy. 80 and stop in every town they come to. There is something different in every community along the way—be it Terrell, or Wills Point, Edgewood, Grand Saline, Mineola, Hawkins, Big Sandy, or all the way to Marshall.

Now some may ask about Canton, or Van, or Winona or Waskom—and yes, these are great stopping places, too—but these towns are on the Interstate (I-20), and if you really want to take a Sunday drive to "see" Texas, I always recommend staying off the interstate highway system when you can.

If you do a nostalgic one-day or overnight trip on U.S. 80 east of Dallas, one "fer-sure" stop would be Edgewood, population 1,517, in Van Zandt County. It's growing like a lot of communities near the Metroplex, and more and more people commute to Dallas from the

"Old Town" in the Edgewood Heritage Park Museum includes a vintage barber shop and general store.

Log houses with picket fences make yesteryear come alive in Edgewood Heritage Park.

Edgewood-Wills Point area. But it's still "Small Town, Texas," and it is probably best known by U.S. 80 travelers for its fruit stands all along the highway.

Edgewood also has what they call Old Town. It's located in the Edgewood Heritage Park Museum, and it's an easy left turn and four-block drive off U.S. 80. And it is an "old town," complete with a vintage grocery store-and-service station, two or three old 1800's log houses with knee-high picket fences, barber shop, blacksmith shop, schoolhouse, Tom's Cafe and a gazebo that will take you back in time. Young or old, plan to spend an hour or longer at Old Town—a "museum" that comes alive.

From
Linda's notes

Van Zandt County — Canton, the county seat, is famous for its First Monday Trade Days, one of the largest flea markets in the U.S. But it's grown so big, now covering 300 acres, the antiques and arts craft fair now begins on Thursday before the "first Monday" of each month. ...Edom is a cute little town that is going to be another artist colony like Wimberley in Hays County. ...Redland is where the Roseland Plantation stood in 1854. It still has a church and two beautiful homes on the plantation estate. ...The county is full of cemeteries!

WOODVILLE IS ANOTHER beautiful East Texas town, in the deep piney woods of Tyler County, and home of the Alabama-Coushatta Indian Reservation, established in the 1850's by Sam Houston after Texas had been admitted to the U.S. as a state.

Like Edgewood, Woodville also has a Texas heritage-style museum, called the Heritage Village Museum, about a mile west of town. While it resembles "Old Town" in Edgewood, with many of the frontier-type buildings you'd find in an 1880's era town, it also has a syrup mill, an old whiskey still, a jail (that goes along with the whiskey still exhibit, huh?), and a log cabin built in 1866 that was occupied as a home for more than 95 years. It has since been restored and features hand-made pegged windows and wood door hinges oiled by bacon rind.

The fact that Linda and I have visited the Heritage Village Museum three times—and we'll do it again soon—is testimony to the lure of this fascinating historical setting. But there is another reason for our

The Heritage Village Museum in Woodville is also home to the Pickett House Restaurant and true country cooking, boarding house style.

many visits here. And that is the Pickett House Restaurant, housed in an old schoolhouse on the village grounds. It's one of those "pay one price, eat all you can eat" places. Great country cooking, with the food served boarding-house style.

The dining area is set up with long tables that will seat up to eight or more folks, and every one shares family-style. When you run out of mashed potatoes, green beans or fried okra, just raise your empty bowl and they'll bring another refill. But you do have to get up and get your own drink, be it water or ice tea (sweetened and un-

From
Linda's notes

Tyler County — I think God used a paint brush to create Tyler County. ...Peachtree Village at the camp features a gorgeous old 1912 church with a large painting of a river baptism over the pulpit. ...The whole town of Woodville is a bird sanctuary. ...Former Governor Allan Shivers' Library and Museum is in a restored Victorian home in Woodville.

159

sweetened) and something that is unique in today's world of diet what-ever—cold buttermilk! Pitchers full of cold buttermilk! Some of us gulped down buttermilk as a kid, some may have tasted it for the first time, but it's one thing that salivates the gastronomic juices for me every time I think of the Heritage Village Museum.

IN A LONG-WINDED chapter on museums, one would surmise that we would save the "best" for last. That might not be the case, however, for it is near impossible to figure which of the little museums off Main Street Texas is our favorite. What is "best" in my opinion might not be Linda's favorite. Nor might it be yours. In these cases, I rely on my Baskin-Robbins philosophy of life. There is a reason why Baskin-Robbins offers 31 flavors of ice cream, for there is a great variety of taste in our land, and everyone of those 31 (or is it now 32?) flavors is the best to someone. But...

Up in the Panhandle of Texas, in Carson County, in the town of Panhandle, there is the Carson County Museum and the Square

House Museum—all on one grounds known as Pioneer Park. The Square House Museum was built in 1887, the first house in Panhandle, and just may be one of the most attractive small museums in the state— depicting through displays and dioramas the history, natural history and art of the Texas Panhandle.

Some brothers from St. Louis moved to Panhandle about 1888, and they moved lumber by oxcart from Dodge City, Kansas, to build a perfectly-square white-frame house for their NRN Ranch.

Besides the Square House Museum, the park has some very interesting sights as well. There's an old locomotive bell, a Santa

The Square House Museum in Panhandle, Carson County, includes a true "square house" built in 1888 from lumber brought in by oxcart.

Fe caboose, old plow and farming equipment, a bank, and a blacksmith shop with a power-driven ax sharpener. There's an 1887 windmill, an early-ranching barn, two art galleries plus an exhibit of various Texas Flags, and a reconstructed pioneer dugout and a "half-dugout" home.

The dugout design was a popular style throughout the South Plains which was—and is, of course—an endless sea of grass with no native timber or stone with which to construct a "normal" above-ground house. Because it was "dug" into ground, or perhaps partially built above the landscape, it was cool in the summer and warm in the winter months. This was the way ranch houses were built in the 1874-1888 era, else the rancher had to drive their wagons some 300 miles just to find timber and lumber.

We learned, in fact, that the half-dugout houses often had an extra room—a guest room, for the school teacher or parson who

161

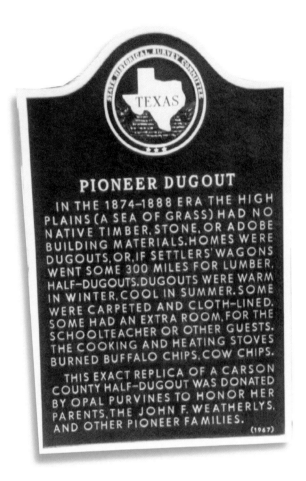

A half-dugout house, on display at the Square House Museum, was a popular ranch house on the South Plains due to lack of timber.

might be passing by late in the day, and the cooking and heating stoves burned either cow chips or buffalo chips.

If you're a history buff, especially a Texas history buff, this is the Garden of Eden of Texas Pioneer lore—yes, miles off the beaten path; yes, just like the little off-Main Street museums in Bigfoot, Rosston, Turkey, Pecos and Stillwell Crossing—a place where

history seems to come alive, so long as you make it on the right day, at the right time of day. If you do, and you make them all, then you can write a book about Texas museums.

And when you do, I'd like to have a copy. ✪

DOAN'S CROSSING— Historical places can be every bit a classic museum unto themselves. These would be places like the Alamo—both the real one in San Antonio and the replica in Brackettville. When you visit both places, they are truly museums in their own right.

Another might be Doan's Crossing, Wilbarger County, about 20 miles north of Vernon on U.S. 283. There you will find a historical marker between two monuments. The granite monument on the right says "Doan's Crossing On Red River. The Western Texas-Kansas Trail, 1876-1895. Six million cattle and horses crossed here."

Under the informative inscription was a quote by Will Rogers, and it's a grammatical humdinger: "You don't need much monument if the cause is good; it's only these monuments that are for no reason at all that has to be big." Quote, unquote.

The state historical marker tells the story of Doan's Crossing, a major route for cattle drives on the Western Trail, reaching from far South Texas to Dodge City, Kansas, in the 1870's and 1880's. About 1876, the marker notes, trail bosses began herding cattle across the Red River. In 1878, Ohio native Jonathan Doan and his nephew, Corwin Doan, established a trading post near the crossing (still standing, by the way) and they began recording the passage of hundreds of thousands of cattle

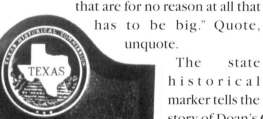

DOAN'S CROSSING

A MAJOR ROUTE FOR CATTLE DRIVES KNOWN PRIMARILY AS THE WESTERN TRAIL DEVELOPED FROM FAR SOUTH TEXAS TO DODGE CITY, KANSAS, IN THE 1870s. ABOUT 1876 TRAIL DRIVERS ALONG THE ROUTE BEGAN CROSSING THE RED RIVER NEAR THIS SITE. IN 1878 OHIO NATIVE JONATHAN DOAN ESTABLISHED A TRADING POST NEAR THE CROSSING AND BECAME THE FIRST PERSON TO PERMANENTLY SETTLE IN WILBARGER COUNTY (ORGANIZED IN 1881). IN THE EARLY 1880s HE AND HIS PARTNER/NEPHEW CORWIN F. DOAN RECORDED THE PASSAGE OF HUNDREDS OF THOUSANDS OF CATTLE ALONG THIS RIVER CROSSING WHICH BECAME KNOWN AS DOAN'S CROSSING. (1973)

Two granite monuments and a historical marker at Doan's Crossing pays tribute to the passage of six million cattle and horses across the Red River from 1876-1895.

along the river crossing. And it soon became known as Doan's Crossing.

The second large granite monument, to the left of the historical marker, shows the various brands of cattle that crossed the Red River here. It stands in front of a classic five-rail split-log fence, and beyond that a bluff that shows miles and miles of mostly Oklahoma.

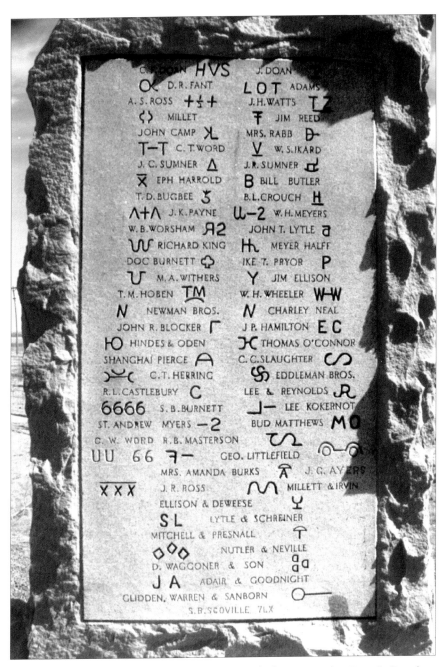

A monument highlights many of the cattle brands that crossed at Doan's Crossing.

166

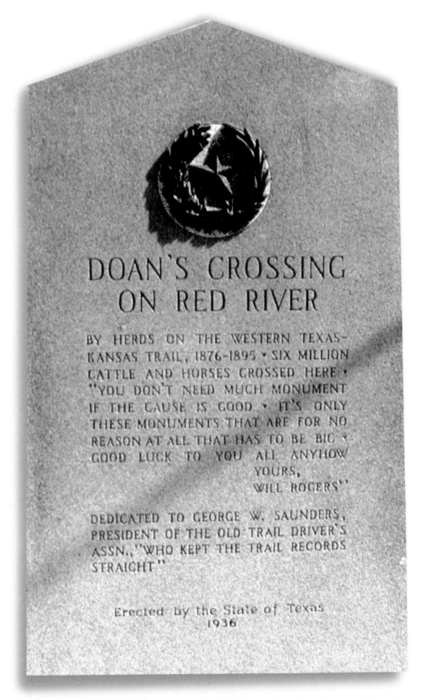

DOAN'S CROSSING ON RED RIVER

BY HERDS ON THE WESTERN TEXAS–
KANSAS TRAIL, 1876-1895 • SIX MILLION
CATTLE AND HORSES CROSSED HERE •
"YOU DON'T NEED MUCH MONUMENT
IF THE CAUSE IS GOOD • IT'S ONLY
THESE MONUMENTS THAT ARE FOR NO
REASON AT ALL THAT HAS TO BE BIG •
GOOD LUCK TO YOU ALL ANYHOW
                        YOURS,
                        WILL ROGERS"

DEDICATED TO GEORGE W. SAUNDERS,
PRESIDENT OF THE OLD TRAIL DRIVER'S
ASSN.,"WHO KEPT THE TRAIL RECORDS
STRAIGHT"

Erected by the State of Texas
1936

Will Rogers added his humor to the 1936 marker that denoted Doan's Crossing.

The Potts old homestead in the Shirley community, Hopkins County.

CHAPTER SEVEN

Nobody Home

*T*here is an image of Texas that still haunts me. It is not something that I thought much about before Linda and I took off on our Great Journey of Texas. But it soon became a testament of our times as we began to take photographs of bygone-era buildings along the back roads—particularly old homes and old barns. These remarkable relics had one thing in common: they were abandoned, left to the winds of change and the whims of history.

You can play a mind game with these places. Every one has a story to tell, and yet, for many of us, their story is untold. For when you don't know the facts, you can only fill in the blanks yourself. How old was this old house, the one with the falling-in front porch? Who built that old weathered barn with the fancy door that is half off its hinges? How many families called that two-story farm house "home," the one surrounded by shade trees and now shrouded in honeysuckle vines? What were some of their success stories? What caused these places to be abandoned? And how long ago?

Again, these were questions that popped into our minds as we took another snapshot of another place that might have reminded us of our kinfolk's farm or old homestead. In truth, we really didn't seek to find the answers.

And yet, what started out as simply taking photographs of interesting relics of rural Texas began to take on a much bigger life—

Beyond the grave (foreground) of my grandfather, Papa Morris, is the Shirley Baptist Church.

life in the long-forgotten era of the early 1900's—especially the 20's, 30's and 40's—when families did things together, when they worked from sunup to sundown, barely able to scratch out a living, but living like the only worry in the world was whether it would rain tomorrow.

Our fascination with old farm houses and barns was inspired by a photo that I happened to take while we were visiting a little community known as Shirley, just outside of Sulphur Springs in Hopkins County—the county where I was born and grew up.

Shirley was once spelled Sherley. I know that to be true, because it was the birthplace of my mother, Nora Morris. I knew her old birthplace home no longer stood, nor did much of anything else, but we had to go there to say we had been there. And sure enough, as I had remembered it as a kid, the community of Shirley consisted mainly of the Shirley Cemetery and the Shirley Baptist Church, an old white frame building at the end of a crooked sandy road.

Family reunions are still held at the church in Shirley, I guess because it's close to the cemetery. In the Shirley Cemetery is where my grandfather, Papa Morris, is buried. We took photographs of the church and Papa's tombstone. As we were leaving, Linda said, "James, stop! Look at that. Wouldn't that make a great picture!"

About 100 yards from the church, set back a ways from a 90-degree turn in the road, was an old house with a rusting tin roof that was so heavy, it had caved in on the house itself. The house was surrounded by a barbed-wire fence with a gate. We didn't go through the gate, but stopped long enough to take a photograph of the old house with a fallen roof. It turned out not only to be a great photo—being the "Photo of the Month" at Wolf Camera Store in Garland—but a place, as it turned out, dear to my mother's heart.

One day, while visiting with Mother at the Christian Care Center in Mesquite, I was sharing our travels with her. As you can imagine, it doesn't take much for a mother to be proud of her son, and indeed our travels and photos thrilled her. But on this day, I proudly told Mother we had visited her birthplace and I showed her an 8x10 photo

The old Potts homestead in Shirley was a place dear to my mother's heart.

of the old house in Shirley. I wasn't sure what to expect.

Mother looked at the photo for just a few seconds, then turned to me and said, "Son, was that house right at that hard turn by the Shirley Cemetery?"

I said, "Yes ma'am, it was."

"Well, James," she said, "that was the Potts family's old home."

I shook my head. "I don't think I knew the Potts family," I sheepishly admitted.

"Well, I did," Mother said matter-of-factly. "The Potts used to own and operate the little grocery store in Shirley. They had a granddaughter named Audrey Beall, who was my age, and when Aubrey came to visit, I would go over to that house and play. I guess we were seven or eight years old then."

Now my mother was born in 1909, so that would mean Mother played at that old house back in 1916 or 1917—and she remembered playing there like it was just yesterday, by looking at a photo of a house that was taken 80 years later. I was so surprised that Mother would recognize that old home so quickly and easily. It was like she was still a young child, remembering all the good times when that house didn't have a fallen roofline, and the porch was still a good place for two little girls to play and share secrets on a hot summer day.

With Mother's reminiscing, and a photo that brought back those memories, it was a moment to treasure. It was also a moment that inspired us to take photographs of other old abandoned homes and barns, and to wonder and ponder the stories these old walls could tell.

In reviewing the hundreds of photos we took, it struck me that these could be the very last photographic record of these old deserted structures that once housed the hopes and dreams of another generation.

Following is a collection of some of the photographs we took of old barns and old houses on our journey through Texas. We hope you enjoy not only the photographs themselves, but enjoy thinking about those places in your own life—your grandmother's old house with a creaky front porch swing, or your uncle's farm with an outhouse, where the watermelon patch was a bouncy pick-up ride past the "pig pen."

And when you do, fill in the blanks—the "rest of the story," if you will—of these memorable old places where, when we came calling, nobody was home. ✪

When an old tractor's day is done near Izoro, Lampasas County.

The last remaining landmark in the
Bulcher community, Cooke County.

Even the chickens are gone from this Clay County barn.

Onetime home of the caretaker at the Seward Plantation, Washington County.

Waiting for future growth, near the Los Rios Country Club, Collin County.

A lonely buzzard keeps watch on a hazy Bosque County morning.

A slave family's quarters on the Old South Plantation near Richmond, Fort Bend County.

A homesteader's cabin still stands, hoping the creek don't rise in Guadalupe County.

180

The party's over at this old home near Egypt, Wharton County.

Still holding onto its legacy, near Brushy Creek, Anderson County.

A tractor with a tired look, near Burton, Washington County.

182

A farmhouse is caught up by the changing times, in Duval County.

A traditional square house, barely surviving among the oaks in Liberty County.

Only a little touch-up needed at this sturdy Bastrop County farmhouse.

Folks here must have moo-ved out, a curious bovine seems to say.

The winds of change have crept up on this farmhouse near Nolan, Nolan County.

For sale? For rent? In Nacogdoches County, a handyman's haven.

185

An old gymnasium's time has run out in Toyah, Reeves County.

CHAPTER EIGHT

Tiny Towns &
Unscheduled Happenings

I've often said that some of the towns in Texas we visited were so small that the "Entering" and "Leaving" signs were on the same post, and that some towns were so tiny they were located halfway between "Litter Barrel" and "Resume Speed."

Regardless of a town's size, they are all very interesting in their own way, and most of them provided us with ample photographic

The Loving County Courthouse in Mentone, represents Texas' least populated county.

187

opportunities. No matter the population, whether it's 200 or two (the smallest we found in Texas), a small town's history, and the lifestyles of the few who live there, is very special.

Loving County has the smallest population of any county in Texas. Located between the Pecos River and New Mexico in far, far West Texas, it had a total population of 96 people when we were there. All 96 of those folks lived in or "around" Mentone, the county seat and the only town in the county. With only 96 people, there might be more coyotes than people living in the county. Well maybe, and maybe not. But we do know there are more oil wells. Try 1,100 of them, making Loving County one of the great deep-well oil producing areas in Texas.

As removed as Loving County may be from the population centers of Texas, it was a busy place in the 1860's. Nine miles north of the Red Bluff Dam on the Pecos, a marker denotes the site of Pope's Crossing where emigrants and the Southern Overland (Butterfield) stage headed west. And two miles south of Mentone, there's a marker indicating where a "feeder" road led to the Goodnight-Loving Trail that cattle drivers used to drive their herds to Colorado and Kansas. Yes, Loving County is named for Oliver Loving, the first cattle trail driver from Texas.

From
Linda's notes

Loving County — Loving County is the least populated county in Texas. And Mentone, its county seat, has no water system, no doctor, no lawyer, no hospital, no newspaper, no civic club or cemetery. You wonder: why stop? ...If you're a fan of Lonesome Dove, the classic book and TV series, this would be the place to go. ...The county was named for Oliver Loving, who mapped three major cattle trails, fought Indians, was shot by Indians, and crawled five miles chewing on a glove for sustenance. Tough hombre, tough country.

THERE'S A SPECIAL LITTLE town in our books—Bethany, Texas, or Bethany, Louisiana, depending on where you're from. For the record, Bethany is in Panola County, at least the part of the town that lies in Texas. The town straddles the state line on U.S. 79, and according to the *Texas Almanac*, the population of Bethany is 50. I suspect that must be the total residents who reside on the Texas

The Lickskillet Old Time Store in Bethany is in both Texas and Louisiana.

At the Lickskillet Store, left of the "blue line" is Louisiana; on the right is Texas.

side of the state line.

It must be interesting to live in a town that's in two states. There's an old hardware store in Bethany that must be 120 years old. The Lickskillet Old Time Store is still in operation, still fully stocked with merchandise. On this winter day, there was a pot belly stove to warm up the place, and it was located on a blue line that was painted right down the middle of the store. So what's with the blue line, you ask? Well, when I moved a little to the left of that blue line, I stood in Louisiana.

The hardware store's doors were open the day we were there, but we learned that the store was "officially" closed. However, even when it is officially closed, the store will open if someone needs something. All they have to do is call and someone will "open" the store just to sell an item to meet a need. Now try that in Dallas or Houston or Austin.

SIPE SPRINGS, in Comanche County, is a ghost town. Now does that make the 75 folks who live here "ghosts"? They didn't seem to be ghosts, but if they were, they were very friendly ghosts. Sipe Springs was founded by settlers around 1870 and named, with a somewhat sophomoric approach to spelling, when someone discovered water "seeping" from rock formations at a nearby springs. There's been a controversy in these parts ever since about the spelling of Sipe Springs. Regardless of how they may argue over its spelling, they all pronounce it "Seep" Springs.

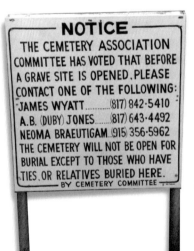

There's nothing here now but a cemetery and a tabernacle. But in 1918, with the

A cemetery notice in Sipe Springs.

The Sipe Springs Tabernacle and Cemetery, for a ghost town, is well maintained.

discovery of oil, Sipe Springs' population mushroomed upwards to 10,000 people, and within a year's time had two hotels, five general stores, two banks, a brick school, several saloons, its own weekly newspaper, and even a semi-professional baseball team. The oil boom was brief, as the oil deposits proved to be shallow, and when both banks failed in 1921 and a fire in 1922 burned a number of buildings, the town began to decline. It became a ghost town during World War I when most of the men went off to war.

The cemetery is well maintained and the tabernacle, built in 1890, is still used for funeral services and homecomings.

A LITTLE BIT OF A SHOCK to us was a town we saw listed in the *Texas Almanac*, the community of Hoover, in Gray County, whose population in 1990 was listed as 5. It is northeast of Pampa, the county seat, and we wondered what five people might do in Hoover. As it turned out, we arrived in Hoover just 90 days after one of the biggest days in its history.

We learned that the town had been sold at auction, to the Attebury

Hoover's population was five, until it was sold to this grain company.

Grain Company, and three of those five residents of Hoover had moved. So now its population was down to two.

THERE ARE A LOT of towns in Texas that aren't even a spot on a map. One that isn't—but should be—is simply called Garvin's Store, in Real County, right at the Kerr County line. It's located where a dot on the map could be pinpointed by map makers. Right at the crossroads of U.S. Hwy. 83 and FM Road 41 is where Garvin's Store sits, a small frame structure with two gas pumps and several pick-up trucks parked in front.

Inside the store, we found freshly-made coffee—"Just help yourself to the coffee if you'd like," the lady behind the counter said—as well as pre-made sandwiches, a few grocery items, and lots of feed. Outside, there were a few ranchers gathered around their pick-up trucks, outnumbered by the phalanx of peacocks that were wandering about as they passed the time of day.

Garvin's Store is more than a store. It is a gathering place. I am sure that the same scene we enjoyed can be found each and every

Garvin's Store is more than a store. It's a gathering place.

day as folks stop here to gulp a cup of coffee, or to grab another sack of feed, or just to gab about the day's work or weather report. It's the only social center in these parts, and the only thing you can see for miles around.

You can't miss Garvin's Store. It is located 27 miles north of Leakey, the county seat. It is also 33 miles south of Junction (Kimble County), 31 miles east of Rocksprings (Edwards County), and 28 miles west of Mountain Home (Kerr County). In fact, there is nothing between Garvin's Store and these four "closest" towns, in four different counties. And it's not even a dot on the map, but should be.

HOW ABOUT A TOWN with a reported population of 20, and the town's not even there? Armstrong is officially on U.S. Hwy. 77, halfway between Mifflin and Rudolph, in Kenedy County, a vast sandy stretch

From
Linda's notes

Kenedy County — The Armstrong Ranch was started in 1852 from a Spanish Land Grant, all 83,219 acres. It is still owned by the descendants of John B. Armstrong, a Texas Ranger who, in 1876, almost single-handedly broke up a band of 25 horse thieves during a gun battle near Carrizo Springs, recovering more than 50 horses. ...The ranch is one of two big ranches in the county.

The "double bump gate" into the Armstrong Ranch, Kenedy County.

of ranchland that borders the Gulf of Mexico. I guarantee that you will not see the town when you pass through. You may not even see the "Armstrong" sign. But if you look close, you'll see a small building on the side of the highway up against a barbed-wire fence. It happens to be a United States Post Office.

The post office is a 10-by-15-foot portable building, and it's not open all day, nor every day. It has part-time hours, basically to serve the 20 "residents" of Armstrong—which is the Armstrong Ranch. The gate into the Armstrong Ranch itself is a "double bump" gate, which sets about 20 yards from the little post office.

A "bump gate," by the way, is one that you can drive up to it, bump it with your front bumper, and it will open because of weights that are situated in order to let it swing out, then back freely. A "double bump gate" is one that operates to let a vehicle go in one way, and out the other. But that is all that you can "see" of Armstrong—no buildings except for a portable, part-time post office and a double-bump gate.

REGENCY IS A NAME that implies importance. It is also the name of a little town in Mills County that sits right on the Colorado River. Regency has a reported population of 25 people and is comprised of one little store, but it also has a bridge—the Regency Bridge. And that does make Regency important in the scheme of things. For the Regency Bridge is a suspension bridge that connects Mills County and San Saba County—over the Colorado River, of course—in far west-central Texas.

From
Linda's notes

San Saba County — San Saba, the county seat, is known for its pecans, which are shipped world wide. ...Regency Bridge is one of two suspension bridges in the county. The other is the Beveridge Suspension Bridge over the San Saba. It's one-half mile north of Wedding Oak, a legendary Indian site where many marriages took place. ...There is a wonderful memorial outside the old school house in Elm Grove, made of wrought iron, listing all graduates' names.

Regency Bridge over the Colorado River is one of Texas' last suspension bridges.

This is scenic country. There is a great view of the hilly countryside as you cross the Colorado River, over the Regency Bridge, and you can park on either side of it and walk down to take a photograph, maybe of a car driving over this old, old suspension bridge. In fact, you may have to have someone in your party drive your own car across for the picture, because this is not a heavily-traveled road. You may be the only one there all during your scenic stop.

There are two ways to get to the Regency Suspension Bridge. One is from the San Saba County side, maybe a mile from FM Road 500. The other way, of course, is the Mills County side, but this will involve a seven-mile drive over a very rough, rocky road off FM Road 574. From either side, it's worth going—if nothing else to see one of the last suspension bridges left in the state.

AS WE TRAVELED TO TOWN after town, there were things that happened to us. Not necessarily troubling things (which we cover in a future chapter, Trouble Along the Way), but what I would call

Isabel Gilmore, left, still runs the cafe in Salt Flat that she helped build in 1929.

"unscheduled happenings."These were events that in some cases were funny, and some not so funny, but they are worth mentioning.

Like the time when we were traveling southwest through the Guadalupe Mountains, and we stopped at Salt Flat in Hudspeth County, located on U.S. Hwy. 180 after it swings down from New Mexico, to have a hamburger.

The Salt Flat Cafe is one of two businesses in town. The other is the Salt Flat Post Office. The lady who runs the cafe used to run an adjoining motel, but it is closed now, and—to keep the "other" business in the family, her daughter is the postmaster. Suffice to say, Salt Flat is all by itself, many miles from anywhere else, out in the "salt flat" region of Texas.

From Salt Flat, we drove south on Texas Hwy. 54, back into the Central time zone, past plain ol' Salt and the state's version of Salt Lake. Driving 55 miles along the Sierra Diablo and Apache Mountains and the 6,432-foot high Victoria Peak, we came to a much larger city, Van Horn, population 2,907, the county seat of Culberson County.

We checked into the motel at Van Horn, and went to the Smokehouse Restaurant for dinner. Now the Smokehouse Restaurant is located next to the Smokehouse Auto Museum, full of restored classic cars from the early 1900's to the '60's. The restaurant itself is very neat, owned by a nice gentleman by the name of Mitch Van Horn, whose family name has no connection to the city of Van Horn.

As we walked into the Smokehouse Restaurant on this particular evening, it was very busy. In fact, it was near capacity. They had only two young women waitresses serving three sections, as well

From *Linda's notes*

Salt Flat — The Salt Flat Cafe & Store was owned by Isabel Hammock Gilmore. Her grandfather, Ed Hammock, homesteaded the land in 1900, got a post office there in 1901-02. She and her husband built the cafe/store in 1929, and then a "tourist court" (early-day name for motel) when U.S. Hwy. 180 was still a dirt road. In 1960, a winter storm with temps reaching minus-25° below ruined the plumbing and they had to close the motel. They live in what was the store and still run the cafe. ...The Greyhound Bus stops at the cafe to load and unload packages and freight. ...Isabel has a photo of Amelia Earhart when she landed her plane behind the store in 1931.

Linda visits with Mitch Van Horn and his collection of vintage cars in Van Horn.

as serving as the "hostess" and the cashier. It was obvious, as we waited to be greeted and seated, that they were having a hard time keeping up. Shortly after we sat down, we noticed one of the waitresses took off her apron and walked out the front door. So now there is only one to run this entire business that was full of hungry patrons, including Linda and I.

I got out of the booth and walked over to the one remaining waitress who was trying her best to serve every one, and told her we would be happy to help if we could.

"I can use all the help I can get," the grateful lady replied.

So for the next half hour or so, Linda and I started greeting people, sitting them down at their table, getting silverware and water, and taking their orders. One table was a party of six or seven members of a college tennis team, and they had been sitting there a long time. A more mature member of the group, surely the coach, grabbed me by the arm and asked: "Sir, do you think there is any way we can be waited on here tonight?"

I told her: "Yes, you can, but only if all of you order the same thing."

And they did—they all ordered hamburgers with french fries and Coca-Cola's—and I was able to take care of them, and I assume they enjoyed their meal.

While we were helping out, the owner, Mitch Van Horn, came in to see what was going on. We explained how we had volunteered to help the one waitress who was left to handle the evening's large crowd. He explained he had just come from a parent-teachers meeting at the Van Horn High School, and saw one of his waitresses at the meeting, and wondered who was watching the store. We later found out that the reason the other lady had removed her apron and left the restaurant and her job was due to the fact her daughter was in the school program at the PTA meeting and she was not going to miss it. You don't see such dedication now-a-days—maybe it was "dedication" in one way, not so much in another—but it gave us a chance and opportunity to serve as a waiter and waitress in a very nice restaurant that we would highly recommend to anyone heading through Van Horn in this sparsely-populated mountainous stretch of Interstate 10 in far, far west Texas.

From Linda's notes

Culberson County — Next to the Smokehouse Restaurant in Van Horn is a museum (free to restaurant patrons) where you can stroll through the private collection of vintage cars. The collection is owned by Mitch Van Horn, owner of the restaurant. ...Van Horn, the county seat, is very historic. It was a stop on the Old Spanish Trail in the mid-1800s ...Lobo is a ghost town with a service station and motel, both closed. It was "for sale" when we visited.

A LITTLE TOWN OF Toyah is off Interstate 10 in Reeves County, but is virtually a ghost town with no businesses, no paved streets, and just a few homes. Buildings that once served as businesses are closed and deteriorating, collecting tumbleweeds instead of dollars. And it provided us with a rather unusual experience.

At the back end of town, there is a very large school-type building. I commented to Linda that I could not believe a town this small had a school that large. Linda said she didn't think the building was a school, but rather a gymnasium. But why just a gym? It was still too

The old gym at Toyah, Reeves County, was deserted—except for 5,000 rattlesnakes!

big for a small town. Regardless, Linda wanted to check it out, because she was sure it was a gymnasium, and she was greatly intrigued by its architecture. I told her to go ahead—and I stayed in the Suburban to catch up on some paper work.

Linda stayed inside the old building for 20 minutes or longer. When she came back to the car, she told me all about what she had seen— still declaring that this was an old gymnasium, whose floors had partially caved in. And so when we got back to the highway, we stopped at a gas station to gas up and get a cold Coca-Cola. While we did that, I started chatting with the young man who was working there at the gas station.

"Tell me about that old school-type building on the backside of town," I asked the young fellow. "Is that a school or a gymnasium?"

"Oh, sir," he replied, "that's a gymnasium. The school that was there has been gone for many years. But what ever you do, do *not* go inside that building!"

"Why not?" I inquired, knowing that Linda had done just that. "Will they arrest you and place you in jail? Will they shoot you for trespassing?"

"No sir," he said, "but I warn you, there is no less than 5,000 rattlesnakes in the basement of that building."

Well, I went back to the car and told Linda that I had "good news" and "bad news." "The good news is that you were right, that building was a gymnasium. The bad news is, you had lots of company."

WE WERE DRIVING through Pecos County one bright sunny Saturday afternoon and came into the little community of Coyanosa, on Farm-to-Market Road 1776, and noticed on the right side of the road a 20-foot-long brush arbor and three guys busily cooking brisket and *asado* (pork chili). They had three large wash pots hanging over some well-built fires, yet there were no other people around and the strange scene out in nowhere caused us to stop and find out what was going on.

In Coyanosa, Pecos County, cooks preparing for a wedding of 300 fixed us some brisket and pork chili "to go."

We introduced ourselves and found out they were preparing a meal for a wedding. The wedding was scheduled to take place in about an hour and a half. And they were expecting more than 300 to attend. Sure enough, while we were there, pick-up trucks started rolling in and cowboys and cowgirls in their Saturday Night best—you know, blue jeans, white shirts, elaborate bolo ties, cowboy hats and boots—began to gather.

Everyone invited us to stay. We appreciated their kind offers, but explained that we needed to keep going, that we had more places to go before sundown. Finally accepting the fact we were busy folks on another mission, they did the next best thing. They fixed up one *mucho grande* doggie bag—some great beef brisket and pork chili—and we added a loaf of bread down Fort Stockton way to truly enjoy the festive fruits of their hard labor. Today, every time we think of barbecue, we think of the brush arbor along a wide spot in the road, out in a far-away place called Coyanosa, population sometimes 300.

JUST THINKING ABOUT those tender morsels of meat we enjoyed at the wedding cookout in Coyanosa brings back other memories—those fabulous places where we enjoyed some great meals along our 135,000 mile trek around Texas.

One of my favorite dinner-time experiences on the back roads of Texas just happened to occur on a Thanksgiving Day. We were in Rusk County, north of the county seat of Henderson, on Farm Road 782. We had reached the top of a short hill and came across the C. E. Rogers & Son Store, a small service station-feed store-grocery store-and-meat market all-in-one enterprise that was over 100 years old.

There was one person inside working and we decided, for this one Thanksgiving meal, to get some Vienna sausage, maybe some good ol' American baloney, a slab of cheese, a package of crackers, and some drinks—and eat our Thanksgiving meal on the road. Linda started shopping for the supplies we needed and I took on the job of

C. E. Rogers & Son Store in Rusk County—home of "cracker-jack" service.

looking for the crackers. I found a regular cracker box—one that contained four sleeves of crackers, which I knew we wouldn't need as we couldn't eat that many—so I kept looking.

The man working behind the cash register came over and asked if he could help me find something, and I told him I wanted some crackers but not a whole box full.

"So, how many do you want?" he asked.

"Well, I was hoping to find a small package, with maybe one sleeve of crackers," I replied.

"If you just want one sleeve, just open that box and take one of those packages out," he said.

"That's very kind," I said, "but I can't do that. That would ruin a box of crackers."

"Don't worry about that," he replied. "Somebody will buy it. There's always folks that just want one, two or maybe three sleeves of crackers. It's not a problem."

What a philosophy! What a lesson in serving the customer! We got our one sleeve of crackers, and our other dinner fixin's, and had one of the most unusual but tasty Thanksgiving meals that we will never forget.

ON ONE OF OUR TRIPS to the northern part of the state, we went into the little town of Turkey, southeast of Amarillo. This is a town of 531 people in Hall County, best known for being the home of Bob Wills, the famed fiddler and "King of Western Swing" star of country-western music. And on Bob Wills Day, held on the last Saturday of April, you can't find a place to stay in Turkey—with crowds ranging from 10,000 to 15,000.

We always enjoyed staying at the old Turkey Hotel in Turkey, about the only thing operating in the downtown area. It was built in 1927— and nothing has changed. Most of the 15 rooms share a bathroom

"down the hall," and the old iron beds in the rooms (and also the bathtubs down the hall) are small—or at least not big enough for lanky guys like me. In fact, when I casually mentioned that I was 6-foot, four inches tall and couldn't fit in one of their beds, the clerk apologized, but reminded me that "when the hotel was built in 1927, there was no such thing as a 6-foot 4-inch cowboy."

There are no keys in the hotel, period— not just to the rooms themselves, but to the front door as well. The room doors do lock from the inside, but not from the outside. And we were reminded there would be "no one on duty after 10 o'clock" at the front desk. Did I mention this old historic hotel hasn't changed in 70 or so years?

Sign entering Quitaque tells you how to pronounce their town in Hall County.

The Sportsman Cafe in Quitaque is so popular, it doesn't need a sign.

It was the middle of the day when we arrived, and I was hungry. As there is no restaurant in the hotel—although they do serve breakfast (it operates as a bed-and-breakfast)—I asked where we might find a bite to eat. Our hostess told us there really wasn't a place in Turkey, but we could drive about 12 miles over to Quitaque, pronounced "Kitty-Quay," in Briscoe County. And she mentioned the Sportsman Cafe.

We drove to Quitaque, which was originally a trading post and stagecoach stop, and didn't see the restaurant she recommended. So we drove back through town and still didn't see anything that indicated it was the Sportsman Cafe or a restaurant by any other name. I was even hungrier by now, so we took another drive down the main street (Texas Hwy. 86), and still no restaurant, so we headed back to Turkey. We saw a lady working on her yard just outside of the Quitaque city limits, so we decided to stop and ask if she knew where this place was.

"The Sportsman Cafe? Oh, yes—it's a great place to eat," the local lady told us.

"Well, ma'am, where is it?" I asked, my starving stomach churning in turmoil. "We've gone through town about four times, and I never saw a sign."

She replied, "Hell, man, they don't have a sign. Everybody knows where it is."

Thanks to her instructions, we did find the Sportsman Cafe—a small, unmarked roadside outpost, surrounded by several pick-up trucks with dogs in the back (as you know, good ol' cowboy dogs never leave the back end of a pick-up) and even a few horse trailers. It should have been evident that "this was the place."

When we walked in the front door, we found ourselves smack in the kitchen, where the tin ceiling was drooping a little, a hot huge oven cooking away. We passed through the kitchen to a back room with tables covered by oil-cloth table coverings and a lot of folks enjoying an early-evening dinner. Even before we could get settled down with our menus, the owner came over with a muffin pan of freshly-baked hot rolls and butter.

Our waitress arrived, and while she did not speak English, she was able to take our order. My chicken-fried steak was about as good as they make in Texas. Maybe the best I've ever had. We have gone back through Quitaque several times since, just to eat a good ol' "chicken-fried" or a hamburger (again, maybe the best hamburger I've ever eaten) and enjoy the hot rolls.

We later learned that the Sportsman Cafe was written up either in *Texas Monthly* or *Texas Highways* magazine for having the "best fajitas in Texas." Need I say more?

ON THE FAR WESTERN side of Texas, in Hockley County, we left the little town of Sundown—in fact, it was just about high noon—and drove west through a pretty good sand storm to Cochran County, near the New Mexico border, and north to Morton, its county seat. Now I used to think Morton was an up-and-coming rodeo town, but

Two "non-talkative" customers dine at the DQ in Morton, Hockley County.

on this day, it looked run-down. Very few businesses were open or operating. But there was a Dairy Queen, and sometimes that marks a town as being hip and with it.

I was ready for a cup of coffee, and so was Linda, so we stopped. When Linda and I walked in, there were no other customers except for a young couple in the first booth to the left. He was wearing a cowboy hat, glasses, and leaning over a big soda with straw. The girl across the table also had a drink—I guessed it was a milkshake due to the shape of the cup—and she was also staring down and not saying a word. I didn't think too much about it at first, and we both got our cup of coffee.

When we got up to leave, I noticed that the young couple at the front table were both still staring down, motionless, not having changed their position all the time we had been there, and having no conversation at all. It naturally bothers me to see two young people so concerned with life that they can't talk, and so—being a bit more nosey than I should have been—I moseyed close to their table. To my surprise, I found both were mannequins—well disguised mannequins—and I'm sure they were still there, saying not a word, when the sun went down that day in Morton.

The next time you stop at the Dairy Queen in Morton, check to see if they are still there. And don't be surprised if they don't look up.

MULESHOE, THE COUNTY seat of Bailey County, has a population of about 4,453, and yet it also has its own television station. As you can imagine, it is extremely rare for a small Texas town to have a TV station—but this one is very successful. It is owned and operated by Magann Rennels, and it is located at her downtown home, in an upstairs room. Folks refer to it as simply Channel Six.

In the early mornings, Channel Six will provide its subscribers today's headline news, upcoming events, obituaries, family reunions, personal items like anniversaries, birthdays, engagements—just about anything and everything that is happening around Muleshoe. Channel

Channel 6 in Muleshoe offers news and advertising from Texas' most unique TV station.

Linda visits with Magann Rennels (right) about her Channel 6 operation in Muleshoe.

Six even films some of the big events like Friday night football games and class plays. And Channel Six also includes local advertising.

Now, the advertising is something to behold. You can see ads on Channel Six from such places as Rosemary's Diner, the local feed store, Red's Service Station, a dress shop, and so on—and sometimes you will see a hand go on the screen, removing one of those ads to replace it with another. As we learned, these ads are scheduled to run for an hour or two each day, at certain times of the day, then it comes time for another advertiser, who has scheduled for its business to be "aired" for the next time period.

These ads are basically printed information on cards—about the size of a filing card—placed on a cylinder that revolves in front of a camera, thus "advertising" on Channel Six. When it is the "advertising hour" (versus the "news" hour) there is also music—ranging from country and western, to gospel, light rock and golden oldies—

covering the spectrum of musical interest for Muleshoe's viewing and listening pleasure.

Needless to say, Magann had heard that we were in town. She found us, invited us to her TV station, and then interviewed us for more than an hour. I don't know to this day if we were "live" or if she showed the interview on a delayed basis, but it was a unique experience—sort of a fore-runner of this book, our 15-plus minutes of fame, in a unique place called Muleshoe, on one of Texas's most unique TV stations, Channel Six.

MASCOTS— Mascots are a great identification for the schools and the teams they represent. They are also a symbol of civic pride in their communities.

Now I was a Bobcat. Linda was a Lion. I attended Pleasant Grove High School in a rural area near Dallas—the Pleasant Grove Bobcats! Linda went to and graduated from Greenville High School, Hunt County—the Greenville Lions! So when we think of mascots, we think of Bobcats and Lions. And these images also bring up other mascots—Bears, Eagles, Longhorns, Mustangs, Tigers—all popular as mascots go. But not

The Hutto Hippo in Hutto, Williamson County.

The Swifts and Swiftettes win big in Nazareth, Castro County.

all mascots are that simple. Not in Texas.

We came across many unusual mascot names as we traveled to every town in Texas. As we entered each of these towns, we knew right off what the mascot of the local high school team was because there would be a billboard just outside of town—like the one outside of Winters, Runnels County, that proclaimed this was "Winters Blizzard's Country." Or there would be a sign just inside the city limits, like in Muleshoe, Bailey County, "Home of the Muleshoe Mules."

There were water towers, professionally painted, like the one in Lewisville, Denton County, "The Lewisville Farmers," and the years they were the state champions in football.

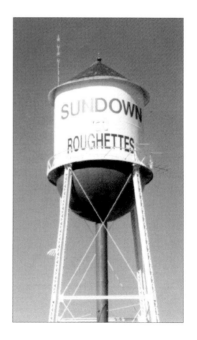

Sundown loves their Roughettes as well as their Roughnecks!

211

In downtown Hutto, Williamson County, there is a large plastic statue of a hippopotamus—yep, home of the Hutto Hippos. In the Fisher County town of Rotan, they root for the Yellowhammers. (What's a yellowhammer? It's a woodpecker.)

We also discovered that many schools have two mascot names—one for the boys team, one for the girls team. Poth, in Wilson County, proudly promotes the Pirettes, the girls basketball team, along with the Pirates, the boys team. Nazareth in Castro County is built around a Catholic church, with a basketball goal in just about every yard, and this is the home of the Nazareth Swifts and Swiftettes—both perennial basketball champs in Class B play. And in Sundown, Hockley County, one side of their town's water tower says "Sundown Roughnecks," and the other says "Sundown Roughettes." Ditto in Levelland, also in Hockley County:

HOME OF THE CUERO "FIGHTIN'" GOBBLERS

- 1970 STATE FINALISTS
- 1971 STATE FINALISTS
- 1973 STATE CHAMPS
- 1974 STATE CHAMPS
- 1975 STATE FINALISTS
- 1984 QTR. FINALISTS
- 1985 STATE FINALISTS
- 1986 STATE FINALISTS
- 1987 STATE CHAMPS
- 1988 STATE CHAMPS
- 1988 QTR. FINALISTS
- 1993 STATE FINALISTS

Inset: Spurettes, not Dogettes. Above: Cuero gobbles up state titles.

So what's a Wampus Cat? Winners in Itasca.

the Lobos and Loboettes.

Rio Hondo, Cameron County, had an average boys mascot name—yea, Bobcats!—but the girls are called the Bobettes. The Spur Bulldogs in Dickens County had another name for its girls team—not the Bulldogettes, but the Spurettes.

All across Texas, many mascots began with the same letter as the town—the Dumas Demons, the Munday Moguls and the Van Vandals. But there were some that just have to be mentioned because of their clever uniqueness—Crane Golden Cranes, Cuero Gobblers, Falfurrias Fighting Jerseys, Freer Buckaroos, Knippa Rockcrushers, Pampa Harvesters, Paul Pewitt Brahmas, Port Lavaca Sandcrabs, Robstown Cotton Pickers, Roscoe Plowboys, Tivoli Redfish, Trent Gorillas and the White Deer Bucks.

And my two favorite: the Itasca Wampus Cats and the Progresso Red Ants!

Meanwhile, Go Bobcats! Go Lions! ✪

The Sam Houston Oak near Gonzales.

CHAPTER NINE

Trees

I think I shall never see
A poem as lovely as a tree.
—Joyce Kilmer.

No, I'm not a tree hugger or a poet. Nor do I profess to know a lot about trees (or poems). Just to show my ignorance, I didn't even know Texas had trees of noteworthy significance—not until Linda and I embarked (no pun intended) on our journey through Texas. I just knew that the Good Lord put out a few good trees in Texas, some which grew to be pretty big and tall, and that was about it.

Now I know better. That is, God really did a masterful job with His tree farm in Texas.

There are many trees that are significant in our great state, either by their size, their location, or by some quirk of history. We found those in our travels, and many more that caught our fancy that may not have a historical marker to tell us it was something to behold.

One unheralded tree that really caught my eye was a big sprawling shade

From
Linda's notes

Aransas County — Cattle baron George W. Fulton built an ornate four-story French chateau, a showplace in its time, between Rockport and Fulton. Finished in 1876, it took four years to build, and included such innovations as central air and hot-and-cold running water. ... Fulton helped promote a deep-water passage and rail service along Copano Bay to market their beef. His efforts helped start the meat-packing industry in Texas. ... Our Lady of the Sea Chapel in Lamar was built in 1858 of oyster shells imbedded in cement. It was shelled by Union troops during the Civil War in 1864.

It's not historical, but this big shade tree in Richland Springs was a good looker. Right?

tree that sits on the school grounds of the Richland Springs schools in San Saba County. It didn't have a marker of any sort, but it definitely was one that I couldn't keep my eyes off of. It was a looker, as they say.

Out on a county road, in Bowie County, there's the Holiness Church surrounded by a lot of trees, and one huge oak tree that apparently had been struck by lightning. It didn't have a single leaf on it, but its gnarly limbs were reaching out everywhere. It was one of those monster trees they always picture in ghost stories. I'm sure it gets a lot of

Right: Gnarly "monster" tree in Bowie County.

216

"The Big Tree" is an immense live oak near Lamar, Aransas County. Right inset: a poem about trees.

second looks from a lot of people. It did for us.

Now those two trees I noted above didn't have a name. But one we really remember did have a name. It was The Big Tree, an immense live oak near Lamar, overlooking Aransas Bay on Goose Island on the Gulf Coast. There are a lot of big oaks and cypress and other such species that make Goose Island State Park a great sanctuary for wildlife—particularly sandhill cranes and Canadian geese—but also tourists and photographers. Here, you can't miss The Big Tree. It is certified as the largest in Texas—and well could be the oldest in Texas, estimated to be a thousand years old.

There's a marker near The Big Tree, with a poem that rambles on a lot, but talks about "... my limbs have shaded generations, my roots have reached for centuries, my children's children surround me ..." and so on. It goes on to tell a story of what the tree hopes to be, and concludes by saying "... since I could not grow green dollars, or silver, or gold, please help me, standing here before me, that we may both grow old together."

Okay, as I said, I'm not a poet, but it was a very poetic description of Texas' oldest if not biggest oak.

SO IS THERE A BIGGER tree than The Big Tree?

According to folks in Rio Frio, Real County, the "biggest" tree in Texas is its own The Landmark Oak, which served as a gathering place for early settlers long before the first school house in the county was built in the 1870s. It's a sight to see, and it's still well-kept thanks to the Friends of the Big

RIO FRIO LANDMARK OAK
STATE CHAMPION
TEXAS ESCARPMENT LIVE OAK TREE 1988
QUERCUS VIRGINIANA VAR. FUSIFORMIS

THIS MIGHTY OAK SERVED THE EARLY SETTLERS AS A SOCIAL, RELIGIOUS, EDUCATIONAL AND POLITICAL GATHERING PLACE.

DURING THE EARLY 1870's A SCHOOL HOUSE WAS BUILT JUST WEST OF THE TREE. IT WAS CONSTRUCTED OF NATIVE CYPRESS LUMBER, AND ITS WALLS WERE FILLED WITH CALICHE.

BETWEEN 1880-1890, N.M.C. PATTERSON LAID OUT THE TOWN OF RIO FRIO USING THE TREE AND SCHOOLHOUSE MOUNTAIN TO THE EAST AS BEARING POINTS.

THROUGH COUNTLESS CENTURIES THIS TREE'S ENORMOUS BRANCHES HAVE PROVIDED SHADE AND SHELTER FOR MANY PEOPLE. WITH OUR LOVING CARE IT WILL BE A PART OF OUR FUTURE.

FRIENDS OF THE BIG TREE

Some claim the Landmark Oak in Rio Frio is Texas' biggest oak. Could be.

A different look at the Landmark Oak, circumference 277 inches.

Tree. It is indeed Big. The circumference of the tree is 277 inches. It's only 52 feet tall but it makes up for that with a 99-foot spread. The Landmark Oak, indeed, may just have the right to carry the title as Texas's biggest oak tree.

Runner-up to the Landmark Oak is probably the Columbus Oak. I guess it's called the Columbus Oak because it's in the city of Columbus, the so-called "City of Live Oaks," in Colorado County. It's another one of those massive, massive trees. This old live oak is estimated to be at least 500 years old. It is 75 feet tall, tall as a nine-story building, and it sits between two residential properties, so it's easy to find.

Columbus is also home to the District Court Tree

From
Linda's notes

Colorado County — Columbus, the county seat, is a treasure-trove of Victorian homes and worth a drive-by view. ...Some of the historic homes are open to visitors during the town's Springtime Festival in May, and its colorful "Christmas on the Colorado" celebration the weekend after Thanksgiving. ...A spectacular stained-glass dome watches over the 1890-era judge's bench in the District Court of the French-motif courthouse.

Columbus Oak

The Columbus Oak is the 2nd largest live oak tree in Texas. This massive tree is 75 feet tall with a trunk circumference of 310 inches. The average crown spread is 112 feet. Our oak is estimated to be 500 years old, or older.

This live oak grows on the Herbert & Callie Necker Estate.

Tender Loving Care Provided By Keep Columbus Beautiful 1995

Above: The Columbus Oak. Right: The District Court Tree in Columbus.

that sits on a median in downtown Columbus. The marker notes that the old oak sheltered the jurors of the Third Judicial District for the Republic of Texas, starting in 1837, before they built their first courthouse out of oak logs.

The Election Oak in Meridian was a polling place in 1854.

ELECTION OAK

ONE OF THREE POLLING PLACES IN FIRST ELECTION HELD AFTER BOSQUE COUNTY WAS ORGANIZED IN 1854. OF 21 VOTES CAST ON THAT OCCASION (AUG. 7, 1854) IN COUNTY, 17 WERE POLLED UNDER THIS TREE. J. K. HELTON WAS ELECTION JUDGE.

OFFICIALS ELECTED WERE: L. H. SCRUTCHFIELD, JUDGE; P. BRYANT, SHERIFF; JASPER N. MABRAY, CLERK; ISAAC GARY, ASSESSOR-COLLECTOR; ARCHIBALD KELL, TREASURER.

IN LATER YEARS, BOSQUE COUNTY OLD SETTLERS ASSOCIATION USED THIS SITE FOR REUNIONS. BY THE COURTESY OF TOM M. POOL, OWNER OF THE LAND. SITE WAS KNOWN LOCALLY AS POOL PARK.

IN MERIDIAN, they named their pride-and-joy Election Oak. When Bosque County was organized on July 4, 1854, they designated three trees around their new county as election poll places. The first election was held on August 2, 1854, and 17 of the 21 votes cast in the county were duly registered under the oak in Meridian—thus earning its place in history as Election Oak.

Some other trees of equal significance include an old post oak in Center City, Mills County, on U.S. 84 east of Goldthwaite, where a weathered sign says it marks the geographical center of Texas. I guess that was true in the old days. Apparently, someone with a

From
Linda's notes

Mills County — About 22 miles southwest of Goldthwaite, on FM 574 over the Colorado River, is the Regency Bridge, built in 1939, and one of the few suspension bridges left surviving and in use in Texas today.

This post oak north of Brady once marked the "geographical center" of Texas. It now looks droopy since a different, more scientific "center" has been so designated.

bit more scientific methods did some survey work and determined that the true "geographical center" of Texas is now north of Brady, in McCulloch County, off U.S. Hwy 377. (For the record, we found a marker on a ranch that claims to be the center of the state, east of Fife.) But the old sign near the old oak in Center City still maintains that is the center of Texas.

Then there's the Fleming Oak. It's located on the southwest corner of the town square in Comanche, which of course is in Comanche County. On that same corner, there's an old log cabin with a marker that tells about Comanche Indian raids in the county in the 1840s and 1850s. The Fleming Oak, I understand, is the only oak left in what was a large grove of oaks around which the town was settled.

Why is it called the Fleming Oak? Well, in 1854, a young kid by the name of Martin B. Fleming was with his father and hid behind this

The Fleming Oak in Comanche faced destruction, but was saved by an armed citizen named Fleming.

old tree during an Indian raid. Years and decades later, when the city began clearing the grove of oaks to pave the square, an old settler—yep, named Martin Fleming—objected by waving a gun and claiming that the tree saved his life during an Indian attack, and that he would protect the tree with his very life. The city relented, and that's why that one oak tree still stands.

Yes, trees in Texas do more than provide a shade.

IF WE NEED TO end our story of trees with a special tree, I reckon that would be the Sam Houston Oak, just east of Gonzales, the county seat of Gonzales County.

Now, most of you Texas history buffs know that Gonzales was the site of the first "battle" of the Texas Revolution, Oct. 2, 1835, when 18 local freedom-loving farmers and townsfolk fought off a brigade of 200

The Sam Houston Oak marks the spot where the Texian Army was recruited to fight for Texas independence in 1836.

Mexican cavalrymen dispatched from Béxar (now San Antonio) to force the surrender of the town's only cannon.

As history recalls, the Texans yelled "Come and take it!" and fired one shot from their small six-pounder— "the shot heard 'round Texas"—and the Mexican troops returned to Béxar without firing a single shot.

The so-called "victory" at Gonzales, followed by the fall of The Alamo in March of 1836, helped General Houston recruit 374 men (and a total of 50 rifles) to join his rag-tag "Texian Regulars," an army of volunteers basically formed under the big oak tree near Gonzales.

As the story goes, General Houston realized he was not ready to do battle with Mexican Gen. Santa Anna to recapture the Alamo, and he did a curious thing by setting fire to Gonzales, then retreating to San Jacinto. It was at San Jacinto, near Houston, where he surprised Santa Anna and defeated a much larger Mexican army in April of 1836, and Texas claimed its independence from Mexico. But the Sam Houston Oak in Gonzales serves as a giant reminder of the struggles our forefathers made to make Texas what it is today.

To find the Sam Houston Oak, go about 10 miles east of town, on U.S. 90A, to County Road 361, then go north about 0.8 of a mile. Just off the road, you'll find this big, big oak tree in front of the McClure Braches Home, a beautiful place once featured in the historical novel, *True*

The McClure-Branches Home, home to the Sam Houston Oak near Gonzales.

Women, and available for tours. The tree has a nice marker that denotes it as the Sam Houston Oak, indeed a Texas shrine—or should be.

Is a tree just a tree? Not in Texas. To our delight, we found these majestic creatures of nature not only beautiful to look at, but they have so much meaning and tell so many stories about our great state of Texas. ✪

Linda is dwarfed by a monster cypress in Utopia, Uvalde County.

CHAPTER TEN

Scatter-shooting

S catter-shooting is how I talk sometimes—you know, say just a little about a lot of things. It's an easy way to cover a lot of subject matter when I'm speaking to a group about our adventures. It's a way of responding to questions involving a lot of topics without covering it like the *New York Times*.

We often get questions like: What is the most unusual name for a town in Texas?

Well, it all depends on what might come to mind at that moment. One day, it might be Ding Dong, a little town in Bell County, population

Ding-Dong is a real town in (where else?) Bell County.

22. And then another day, the town of Iraan in Pecos County, might come to mind. Iraan, you ask?

Yep, Iraan—pronounced "Ira-Ann." If you ever visit Iraan, don't say "Ah-ran," because that's how you pronounce the name of a foreign country, not a red-white-and-blue kind of town in Texas! The folks in Ira-Ann are very touchy about the correct way you call their town. So now you know.

Speaking of Ira-Ann (so you don't think I'm thinking Ah-ran), this little town's claim to fame is that its newspaper, the *Iraan News*, was

Alley Oop, the old cartoon character, has a park named for him in Iraan.

the birthplace of the comic strip character, Alley Oop, the lovable cave man who was the gleam in the pen-and-ink mind of V.T. Hamlin when he worked at the local newspaper in the 1930's. And there's even a park in Iraan called Fantasyland, dedicated to Oop and his pet dinosaur pal, Dinny.

AFTER WE DROVE to just about every nook and cranny of Texas, everyone wants to know what our favorite place in the state might be. The answer to that is easy and always the same: Big Bend.

I am not speaking just of the Big Bend National Park—so big and beautiful it's hard to distinguish where reality and fantasy begin and end. Even beyond the national park boundaries, there is lots to do and see in the whole Big Bend region. This is one wide-open place of jagged mountains, steep canyons and enormous expanse that truly seems to be untapped, untouched, untainted.

Driving those straight-as-a-crooked-arrow roads in Big Bend, you can travel many miles and not see any human being—just herds of mule deer, flocks of wild turkey, packs of scavenging javelinas and perhaps a single soaring golden eagle that all by itself rules the sky. Towns like Lajitas, Terlingua and

From Linda's notes

Big Bend — The drive down Farm Road 170, along the Rio Grande and the Mexican border, is a must. Beautiful drive ...looking at solid-rock mountains ...rapids in the river ...15% grade descent. ...Saw set of "Streets of Laredo" movie set near Lajitas, filmed there in 1995 starring James Garner. ...Fort Leaton, in Presidio County, was named for Ben Leaton who bought the fort in 1848 and became the first Anglo farmer in the county. The fort was originally established by monks to Christianize the Indians, and is beautifully restored.

The mysterious Marfa Lights get billboard treatment near Marfa.

Part of the movie set for Streets of Laredo, *located near Lajitas.*

Valentine are miles apart but interesting places in their own right.

Naturally, there are some special places in Big Bend Country that have always fascinated us. The mysterious Marfa Lights are just about the most intriguing natural phenomena anywhere in the world. Yes, the flickering balls of light that flash-dance down the Chinati Mountains near Marfa are really there. We've seen them many times. If you're curious about what they are all about, it's best that you do a little research—because I can't tell you why they're out there performing their magical display sometimes, but not all the time. Suffice to say, they've been around since they were first "discovered" in the late 1800's—long before electricity, long before cars, long before

laser shows—and probably long before they were discovered by man.

ANOTHER BIG BEND treat that was fascinating for Linda and I was in the little town of Valentine, on U.S, Hwy. 90 west of Marfa. Valentine doesn't have much to offer in the way of sight-seeing or fast-foot restaurants. It does have a cemetery seen by millions of movie goers in the classic flick, "Giant," and we cover that in the Cemeteries chapter.

The reason we became intrigued and in love with Valentine is probably because of Maria Carrasco, the town's postmaster. She can treat you to something special if you so desire. "Just send your pre-addressed valentine card to me, in care of the post office here, and I will place 'The Sweetheart Station...Valentine, Texas' cancellation stamp on the envelope and mail them for you," she told me. I thought that was a neat touch, and a good idea.

Now, I know that Loveland, Colorado, does the same sort of thing—and according to our good ex-Texas friends Eddie and Linda Hughes, who live up there, that city has been re-mailing Valentine cards for 30 years or more, and sending them all over the world. But that's a Colorado post mark. If you're a true Texan like I am, I'd rather send my little sweetheart Linda a nice card that was postmarked from "The Sweetheart Station" in Valentine, Texas.

WHILE WE'RE STILL scatter-shooting about Big Bend, I need to take a minute or two to say a few words about Alpine. In Big Bend Country, that's a big town. It might not be big when you think of Little Chicago (Dallas) or Big Cotulla (San Antonio), but in these parts, Alpine is big. As I recall, it even has a Dairy Queen *and* a McDonald's.

Cowboy Poet's Gathering in Alpine caters to cowboys young and real (as in real hungry).

There's an event in Alpine held every year that we absolutely love. It's the Cowboy Poet's Gathering, headquartered at Sul Ross State University, that goes on for two grandiose, guitar-thumping days.

Now, these so-called poets are real working cowboys. They may have just moseyed in from a branding session on the range, or put on their Sunday best which usually means a tie and clean boots. Most

Cowboys plunk and sing to the delight of anyone who wants to be entertained.

will act like they're awed to be in Alpine, and the sweat-soaked Stetsons artfully tilted back on their heads probably haven't been removed for days except to doff as a friendly howdy-do to any cute cowgirl who might pass by. These are hard-working cowhands who write their own poetry, and some of these pearls of prose are recited as they plunk their guitars, and some are sung to the delight of dudes like Linda and I who come to be entertained.

At such gatherings, there is lots of merchandise for sale, like

233

western paintings, silver concho belts, and such. Then one night, down at the park, there is a cowboy chuck wagon cookout and for a small price you can get campground coffee and barbecue, and listen to a lot of pickin' and singin' as they sit around, unrehearsed, and recite their home-on-the-range poetry.

The Big Bend Saddlery—a western store icon in these parts—sponsors a cowboy breakfast with pancakes, bacon and biscuits all cooked over an open fire. Also, down at the Sul Ross Blacksmith School, they have an iron-bending demonstration. That's when blacksmithing students make various novelty items out of the same iron ingots that horseshoes are made of. It's neat to watch them work.

Suffice to say, big doings in Big Alpine is worth the price of gas it will take to get there.

Blacksmithing students at Sul Ross State University make novelty items.

ONE LOOK AT THE official state of Texas map, and you'll think there are only three or four roads in all of Big Bend. 'Taint so. One of the unique features of Big Bend is the extensive network of roads. Of course, many are not paved. But folks always ask us what our favorite Big Bend scenic drive is, and I suggest they take U.S. 67 out of Marfa south to Presidio, then follow Farm-to-Market Road 170 to Lajitas and Terlingua.

When we head down to Presidio on U.S. 67, we like to stop at Shafter, a ghost town in the Chinati Mountains, where you can kick around and check out a few historical markers.

The ghost town of Shafter has a few historical markers.

At Presidio, you can almost throw a rock into Mexico. Presidio is a pretty busy place, but for our scenic journey, we need to head south on FM Road 170. You'll drive maybe 50 miles along what is called the Camino del Rio, or the River Road, because it follows the ever-snaking Rio Grande.

Now for all you newcomer dudes to Texas, we never say Rio Grande River. That would be repeatin' yourself. Rio means river. So you don't say River Big River. You just say Rio Grande.

This is the drive of all drives. The good part is that it's all paved. The scary part is that you'll see signs that say "Loose Livestock." Don't be surprised if you come up over a hill and there's three or four horses standing in the middle of the road. They didn't jump over a fence. There just aren't any fences. And, maybe it goes without saying, but make the drive in the day time—not at night.

About 15 miles before you get to Lajitas, you'll come to a roadside pull-off that sits high above Colorado Canyon, which leads into the ever-spectacular Santa Elena Canyon, with sheer 1,500-foot limestone walls. The scenery is spectacular. At Lajitas, the road turns toward the western entrance to the Big Bend National Park, and we recommend that you stop and get out at Terlingua, every chili-lovin' Texans' favorite ghost town.

Terlingua's population is 25. Or was when we were there. It can grow into the thousands when they have such things as world

On the River Road, look out for loose stock. They are slow to respond to honking.

championship chili cook-off events. That may be why it's one of Texas' most famous ghost towns. Thanks to a restaurant and store, along with river guides and outfitters that make their headquarters here, Terlingua enjoys a modicum of prosperity. But the rows of leaning crosses and weathered wooden markers in the cemetery attest to the hard life quicksilver miners had here in the 1880's.

I think if you can make the 65-mile trip from Presidio to Terlingua, you will understand why we think Big Bend is such a national treasure, and one heckuva scenic drive.

A final note: you can enter the Big Bend National Park just beyond Terlingua, at Study Butte, another quicksilver mining town that is littered with abandoned mining shafts and rock ruins that once were the homes of mine workers. Inside the park, there are camp grounds, RV parks and even a 72-room rustic lodge in the Chisos Basin where reservations are needed almost a year in advance.

ENOUGH ABOUT Big Bend. Let's talk about something smaller. Los Ebanos in Hildago County is small. Population is said to be 100. That may be stretching it a bit. It is southwest of Edinburgh, which means it is touching Mexico. Except for us trying to make it to every town in Texas, there normally would be no reason at all to go into Los Ebanos.

This is an old Hispanic town, with more ties to Mexico than Texas. But it does have a claim to fame. It has the last hand-drawn ferry in the United States. This unique little ferry operates every day, going back and forth across the Rio Grande between the U.S. and Mexico. It is totally reliant on manpower. No machinery of any kind is aboard this fascinating little ferry.

The ferry at Los Ebanos is manned by at least three or four men, standing on the side of the ferry,

From
Linda's notes

Hildago County — Los Ebanos was established in 1850. The ferry here is the only government-licensed, hand-pulled ferry on any border of the U.S. It sits across from Días, Mexico. ...A reporter from Associated Press met us in Los Ebanos for a story about our travels. The story went nationwide and we heard from people all over the U.S.

Los Ebanos has the last hand-drawn ferry in the USA.

pulling on a rope-cable that has been swung across the river. This ferry has been in operation for many, many years. And they take cars as well as pedestrians. At maximum, it can hold only three full-size cars. The cost to transport a car is very inexpensive. The cost for one individual going over to Mexico is 25 cents. And *si*, there is a U.S. Customs Office on the American side.

Albert Samos is the captain of the ferry, and he told us that the fellows who were doing the muscle work—pulling on the rope cable, all day long—all live in Mexico. They come to work every morning in a row boat. And they go home at night in a row boat.

There have been some rumors about doing away with the ferry (no doubt initiated by U.S. Customs budget czars), but Captain Samos said there have been some very strong support among *"muy distinguido amigos de Los Estados Unidos"*—especially a vocal woman in Houston, he says—to keep the operation going because it is so historic and so unique. Samos said if any rumors pop up about halting the Los Ebanos ferry, they call their lady friend in Houston and she comes with her "Army" and that's that.

Whether it is cost-efficient or not, the little Los Ebanos ferry probably has done more to improve international relations than NAFTA ever hoped to achieve. That's just my opinion, and if I had a vote on the matter, I'd like to see this little ferry go on and on as long as the hearty men who daily muscle it across international waters can keep it going.

MCDADE, A TOWN OF 300 in Bastrop County, isn't even a wide spot on U.S. 290 between Austin and Houston. That's because it's a little north of the highway. So most folks miss it, and it certainly isn't mistaken for "Tinsel Town" Hollywood. It has an old general store we had heard and read about, which has been around for more than a hundred years, and a historical marker about a famous Revenge Gunfight of 1883.

From
Linda's notes

Bastrop County — Bastrop, the county seat, is a must-see. ..."The Crossing" is a collection of authentic small old homes and buildings developed as a village with shops, restaurants and great cottages to rent. ...The Bastrop Opera House built in 1889 is now a cultural center. ...Bastrop has over 100 historical homes.

McDade in Bastrop County was alive with actors filming a TV movie. The nice two-story building on the right was not made of brick, but rather Styrofoam.

But when you drive into this rustic rural relic with a water tower, you don't expect to see what we saw.

There were lots of vehicles parked along the narrow roads that lead into the so-called downtown area, and a huge vacant area just outside of town—maybe encompassing 20 to 25 acres—and it was solid full of trucks, travel trailers, moving vans and giant "semi" rigs.

We soon learned that they were filming a special mini-series for television in downtown McDade. The travel trailers were where cast members lived while "on location." The large semi-trailers had been used to bring in wagons and surreys and other "Old West" props for the movie. The vans were full of western wardrobe worn by the actors and actresses during the day while they were working.

Like everywhere else we went, we knew if we wanted to find out what was happening we had to get out of the car. That was no easy feat in McDade on this day, because parking was at a premium. We finally did squeeze our Suburban in between a semi and a horse trailer and walked into town.

Now, downtown McDade is a single row of buildings, with a large grassy expanse between the storefronts and the old Southern Pacific Railroad tracks that created this town in 1869. Sure enough, on the left-hand side was the old grocery store that we had heard about. But Main Street had a new look—well, make that an "old" look—for it had been covered by dirt two or three inches thick. I guess you just don't film a western movie on 1930-era pavement.

They weren't filming at the time we walked into town, but many men, women and children in costume were just milling around—the women carrying parasols and rugged-looking men on horseback,

The general store in McDade did a booming business during the days of filming.

waiting for their cue to be a part of another "scene" or "take."

It was surely interesting to see first-hand a small town that probably hadn't seen its heyday since 1879 become a thriving town once again. You can imagine that all of the businesses in McDade, including the old grocery store at the end of town, were thriving while the cast of characters and onlookers spent real money on real things.

About a block away from the old general store, there were two rather nice-looking brick buildings, one three stories tall, and another two floors high. I was quite surprised to see such fine looking establishments in such a small town. I asked a police officer who was assigned to keep a watch on all the festivities what those two buildings were. He looked at me as if I was either stupid, or from out-of-town.

"Sir," he finally said, "they aren't for real. They're made of Styrofoam, and they were made just for this movie." Duh. Sure enough, they were beautiful from the front, just plain-plain from the back. But in the movie, they would look just like a well-to-do bank and an upstanding office building.

I don't recall what the name of the town was in the movie ("True Women," a made-for-TV production based on the book by Janice Woods-Windle) but when the movie-makers left McDade, the two fake brick buildings would be gone, along with the dirt on Main Street, and McDade would be back to being McDade.

But on this day, it was as busy as it's ever been.

SCATTER-SHOOTING in another part of the state, Bosque County is on the edge of Texas' famed Hill Country, a land of noble oaks, pastoral fields of bluebonnets and paintbrushes, and limestone cliffs. Straddling the beautiful Bosque River, the county is undergoing an influx of growth due to folks in Dallas and Fort Worth and Waco wanting a little more elbow space and rolling geography.

In Bosque County, we found something most unusual—although

it isn't something that would make the 10 o'clock news, not even Bob Phillips of WFAA-Channel 8's Country Reporter fame. No, this is pretty small as oddities go, but we still think it is worth mentioning.

In Clifton, down the river on State Hwy. 6 from the county seat of Meridian, we found the county's only operating three-light traffic light. By three lights, we mean red, yellow and green. So what's the big deal about a three-light traffic light? As I said, it's the only one in all of the county. All of the other operating traffic lights in Bosque County are flashing red or flashing yellow lights.

Like I said, it's not something that would make a newspaper headline, but it would make a tantalizing Texas trivia question: What county in Texas has only one red-yellow-and-green functioning traffic light?

By the way, we checked out this fact with a number of folks in the know, and they say as far as they know, that is a true oddity. Of course, there are several counties in Texas that don't even have one three-light traffic light. But only one with one.

SOUTH OF HOUSTON, West Columbia in Brazoria County has a replica of the first capital of Texas, when Texas was a republic. The first capital—a simple one-story frame building—was actually in old Columbia, where West Columbia now sits. Its fame as the first capital lasted for only three months. The capital was moved to the bigger "town" of Houston by none other than the Republic's first president, Sam Houston, because of a lack of "appropriate" accommodations in Columbia. So West Columbia today is an historic place, and many who are interested in the history of Texas make this growing suburb of Brazosport a must travel

From
Linda's notes

Brazoria County — Plantations abound in this county. ...Replica of the first capital of Texas, originally in Columbia, has been restored. ...Under the Masonic Oak Tree, Texas' first Free Masonry chapter was petitioned in 1835. ...West Columbia and East Columbia are great stops for historians. ...Stephen F. Austin died just outside of West Columbia shortly after he had taken oath as the Republic's first secretary of state. ...Varner-Hogg State Park has the last home of James Stephen Hogg, first native-born governor of Texas. ...Saw an old ferrying dock on the Brazos, site of a Cary Nation Hotel.

Replica of the first Republic of Texas Capitol building in West Columbia.

stop on Texas Hwy. 36.

Just east of West Columbia is East Columbia, which sits alongside the Brazos River. You might think that history (and growth) has somehow by-passed this little community. It's population is 95, compared to West Columbia's 4,500 residents. Yet it indeed has historical ties to early Texas. It is one of the oldest Anglo settlements in Texas—established as Bell's Landing in 1824. It began as a major river port and commercial center for Stephen F. Austin, the so-called

The old Sweeny-Waddy log cabin along the Brazos River near East Columbia.

"father of Texas," and was the third of some 300 land grants in Austin's original colony of Anglo families to settle Texas.

East Columbia has a plethora of beautiful old plantation homes that line the Brazos River, and several old log cabins that still remain along the river. The old cotton plantations no longer exist, but the historic homes still do, and you can stand on the banks of the Brazos and almost hear the steam whistles of the grand old paddle-wheelers, *Hiawatha* and *Brazos Belle*, that once plied their way up and down the river to transport cotton and other goods to the seaports of Houston and Galveston.

THROUGHOUT A GOOD part of East and Southeast Texas, some of the state's largest plantations were formed, primarily involved in raising cotton and sugar cane, and many of the old plantation mansions are still around. However, few are still doing that they did best in the antebellum years before and after the Civil War.

In Panola County, we found in the Adams Store community what is left of the old Adams Plantation. This was a huge place, and at one

Tom J. Moore & Sons store still does business on the Rogers Plantation, Brazos County.

time had more than 100 slaves working here. There was a store at the headquarters of this plantation, the Adams Store, where slaves could purchase most everything they needed or wanted.

Now, the Adams Store was a unique store. The only "money" that the store would accept was currency made by the owners of the plantation, and used to "pay" their workers. The old store is still there, but falling into disrepair from years of neglect. And the old brick plantation headquarters house still stands, and one of the descendants of the original Adams family still lives there and still raises cotton. The Adams Store community is east of De Berry and just west of the Texas-Louisiana state line.

Another old cotton plantation that is extremely active is the Rogers Plantation in Brazos County. It's on Farm Road 154, south of Bryan and west of Navasota in Grimes County. The neat little homes that once housed slaves are still used by today's plantation workers — mostly of Mexican-American descent — and they are paid a salary plus having a rent-free house to live in. The Rogers Plantation is a modern version of what the olden-day plantation might have been like.

From Linda's notes

Burnet County — Oatmeal is close to Bertram, which looks like a movie set. Very artsy town, but not yet discovered. I love this town. ...A steam engine goes from Burnet, the county seat, to Austin every Saturday and Sunday for tourists. ...Burnet is a great place to visit, with lots of old buildings and antique stores. ...The Confederate Air Force Museum south of town was really interesting.

TEXAS IS KNOWN for its various festivals (they aren't all held in San Antonio) such as the Watermelon Thump in Luling, the Blackeyed Pea Festival in Athens, the Spinach Festival in Crystal City and the Strawberry Festival in Poteet.

Yet, it was a big surprise to us when we drove through the Hill Country around Marble Falls and came into Oatmeal, on Farm Road 243, in Burnet County. Okay, I'm sure you can guess the rest—yes, this is where the annual Oatmeal Festival is held.

What was surprising to us is that this is a town of only 20 people,

Luling's big event is its Watermelon Thump.

and they not only hold an annual festival, but they have a giant festival grounds for their annual event. In fact, the festival grounds is just about the whole town.

So what might you find in the Oatmeal Festival? Well, if you are a creative type, this may be your chance to enter something fun. All you have to do is create something artistic out of oatmeal. It doesn't mean preparing your favorite dish of flavored oatmeal. This isn't a tasting contest. Entries usually include such creations as a castle, a doll, whatever you think you can create out of oatmeal.

We learned Oatmeal (the community) is really made up of 10 farming and ranching families, and that they put on the festival with

The Spinach Festival is Pop-Eye big in Crystal City.

248

the good people of Bertram, just up the road. So, other than the festival, the town really doesn't exist. But it did once — a post office, two schools, a gin, a general store, and the first and only cheese press in the county. It also once had the only all-black cemetery in Burnet County. But the settlement ceased to exist by the 1920's. One school building, built in 1869, was used as a church as late as 1990 and is marked by a state historical marker.

We also later learned that Oatmeal is Burnet County's second-oldest town. The town was named Oatmeal in 1853 either because it was a botched spelling of Mr. Othneil, who owned the first grist mill in the area, or a translation of the Habermill family who first settled here in 1849. If you know your German, *Haber* is a derivative

The Oatmeal Festival in Oatmeal has little to do with breakfast food.

of the German word *Hafer*, or "oats." So much for your lesson in German today.

SOME OF YOU country-western fans may remember the song sung by ol' Tex Ritter, "Tenaha, Timpson, Bobo and Blair." Those were all stops along the old Southern Pacific Railroad in this forested area of deep East Texas.

If you go to Tenaha, in Shelby County, you'll also come across Texas' shortest highway. We understand this "shortest" highway was built primarily so that the square in downtown Tenaha could be paved. I'm not sure exactly why this was so, but Loop 168 is officially the designation of this honest-to-goodness highway, dedicated in August, 1945. For the record, it stretches for an entire 359 feet—or 0.074

Tenaha in Shelby County was a stop on the old Southern Pacific Railroad.

miles. That's maybe three-fourths of a city block. And so there's another little-known item for you Texas trivia buffs.

"OH, I LOVE Saint Jo," Linda says every time the subject comes up about favorite little towns. It straddles U.S. Hwy. 82 between Gainesville and Nocona in Montague County, with a population of 1,137. It's an artsy kind of town in the middle of ranching country, but it's best known for the Stonewall Saloon, restored from its 1873 days when it was a watering hole along the Chisholm Trail.

It's what I call a relic store—a relic itself, and it sells a lot of relic wares that you'd think were around back in 1873. In fact, the old bar in the Stonewall Saloon is its original bar. As you would expect, there are several bullet holes here and there in the bar room from shootouts inside the saloon.

We learned from the good folks who run the place—officially

Stonewall Saloon in Saint Jo opened in 1873. It's now a museum.

known as the Stonewall Saloon Museum—that Saint Jo was named for Joe Howell, who laid out the town site in 1856. He called it Head of Elm, because it was established on the springs that were the headwaters of Elm Fork of the Trinity River. He was also the fellow who opposed the sale of liquor in town, and so he and his town soon

The old bar in the Stonewall Saloon still has a few bullet holes.

began to be known as "Saint Jo"—though no one seems to know why they dropped the "e" in Joe.

We don't know if Joe Howell, alias "Saint Jo," was around in 1873 when the Stonewall Saloon opened its doors to quench the thirst of travelers along the Chisholm Trail, but the old saloon-museum today makes for a historic stop, and is located on the town square.

SAN PATRICIO IS A small town barely in San Patricio County, very near Corpus Christi. It has some beautiful, stately old mansions from the 1890's and early 1900's that have been restored, as well as a reconstructed 1872-era courthouse when San Patricio was actually the county seat. In fact, little San Patricio has quite a history—being on the Camino Real where it crossed the Nueces River, as well as the east-west Cotton Road where gold-seeking wagon crews would stop to buy goods and drink if they didn't get hijacked along the way.

It is also the site of the famous Battle of San Patricio in early 1836

Rattlesnake races are big in little San Patricio.

when the Mexican Army was making its big push toward San Antonio and the Alamo during Texas' fight for independence.

So there is a lot of history here and a lot of landmarks. And because of that, San Patricio hosts one of the most unusual events in Texas. It is the Annual World Championship Rattlesnake Races, and it is sponsored by the San Patricio Restoration Society as a way to raise funds to preserve the city's landmarks.

Now I don't know if you would make a special trip to San Patricio to see rattlesnakes try to out run one another, but folks around these parts come in by the truckload and fill the grandstands set up especially for this annual event. They also feature booths selling rattlesnake meat and other delicacies. So if you're ever in the area of Corpus Christi or Kingsville, make a detour up Farm Road 666 for some of the wildest action this side of the Rio Grande.

And visit the historic town of San Patricio while you're here.

SCATTER-SHOOTING the state of Texas and thinking about places to stay… People are always asking us "where did you stay?" And we often reply, "We stayed in a lot of places that we would not recommend." Of course, we stayed in many motels that we felt were very comfortable

Historic Gage Hotel in Marathon is a favorite stay-over in Big Bend territory.

and fulfilled the need for a nice overnight rest. But naturally, we have some favorites, too.

Three immediately come to mind, and they are in different areas of the state.

In the Big Bend area, the historic Gage Hotel in Marathon, in Brewster County is a great old hotel, with an upscale restaurant—Cafe Cenizo—that features grilled prime steaks and roasted game. But one reason we liked to stay here: The Hotel's 19 uniquely-decorated rooms don't have telephones or televisions. I like to describe the rooms as being furnished in "early bunk house" decor, making it feel historic, and it is.

Once left derelict, it was fully renovated in 1978 to capture the rich heritage of the cattle industry that was long the lifeblood of this area. Built in the 1920's, it still features the original pine floors and woodwork, but it also features a secluded heated pool and a lush courtyard filled with flowers.

When you stay in the Gage Hotel—it's owners, J.P. and Mary J. Bryan call it "the Gage experience"—you truly get the feel of a time when a breath of fresh air, a night sky filled with stars, and a hot bath was all a cowboy needed to feel alive. Speaking of baths, some rooms have a private bath, and some share a bath. But each room that "shares" a bath has terry-cloth robes available to walk down the hall in style. And if you're a light sleeper, beware the passing of several freight trains that rumble just across the highway from the hotel.

The hotel was started in 1920, and opened in 1927, by Albert Gage as the headquarters for the Alpine Cattle Company which he and his brothers founded. As it turned out, Alfred Gage didn't get to enjoy the success of his hotel very long. He passed away the year it opened.

It is difficult to get reservations here. Marathon is only about 35 miles from the entrance to Big Bend National Park, so it is a busy place with travelers from all across the world coming here. There are other more traditional motels, and even a bed-and-breakfast just behind the Gage Hotel. But the Gage Hotel is, indeed, a great place to stay and we have on many occasions.

From
Linda's notes

DeWitt County — Wildflowers in the springtime are gorgeous in this county. ...In Cuero, home of the Cuero High School Gobblers, they have a Turkey Trot celebration every October. ...The Doll House Cafe is an authentic 1950's diner.

Another favorite is the Turkey Hotel in Turkey, Hall County, not far from Palo Duro Canyon and the Texas Panhandle. We have mentioned the Turkey Hotel several times in this book, which goes to show how much we have enjoyed staying here. It is a quaint, rustic two-story in the heart of a very quiet town.

The Turkey Hotel was built in 1927, and little has changed. Like the Gage Hotel, some of the rooms share a bathroom down the hall. The rooms are furnished in 1927 decor. Linda and I did have trouble sleeping the first night we stayed because the iron bedsteads are a little shorter than my 6-foot 4-inch frame. Of course, the owner of the hotel pointed out to us that when the hotel was opened in 1927, "there were no six-foot-four cowboys." Those old-time bathtubs that sit on four legs are also a challenge for long-legged folks like me.

Turkey Hotel in Turkey has no keys—the way they did things in 1927.

Still, the Turkey Hotel offers great hospitality, and a super breakfast that is part of staying here—about the only meal you can get in town. Every morning, guests in the hotel gather in the downstairs dining area where home-style cooking and homey touches add to the atmosphere of the boarding house era.

And speaking of atmosphere, there is not a single key in the entire hotel. They never lock the front door, and there are no keys to any of the rooms, but you can latch the doors when you are inside your room for security reasons. But if you are out and about and don't get in until late, you can just walk in the front door (after 10 p.m. there will be no one at the front desk), go up to your room, open the door, and go right in. This was the way they did things in 1927, and the way they do things today.

As noted elsewhere, Turkey is the home town of Bob Wills, the "king of western swing," and hosts the annual Bob Wills Reunion on the last Saturday in April when 10,000 to 15,000 Bob Wills and country-western music lovers converge on this little town of only 531 people.

Also high on my list of favorite places to stay is Utopia. With a name like that, it has to be a great place, right? But if you are going to stay in Utopia, in the northeast corner of Uvalde County, there is only one place to spend the night—the Utopia On The River Inn. It is a relatively small place, off Farm Road 187, probably has no more than 15 rooms, and it also operates as a bed-and-breakfast with a large common room where at night you can relax in front of a real-log fire and play dominoes, cards or just read. And shortly after sundown each night, if you look close, you will see several deer roaming around the area.

Naturally, the Utopia On The River Inn sits right on a river—the very fast-moving but shallow Sabinal River—only about 50 feet from your room. The quiet gurgle of cool water rumbling over river rocks adds to the ambiance of this place. The river flows alongside some of

Utopia On The River Inn in Utopia is utopian in every way.

Linda is dwarfed by big cypress trees along the Sabine River in Utopia.

the largest cypress trees I've ever seen. These trees are so big that it would take four people, holding hands, to reach around the girth of their trunks.

When we were there, Karyn and Brian Jones were operating the inn, and Brian went out with some of his Utopia friends on a "hog hunt." I learned that this was a big sport in these parts—there are so many of them that they need to "thin" them out.

So if you're looking for a quiet get-away, and some place where it's a beautiful drive to get there, Utopia is the place.

SCATTER-SHOOTING, I hope, has been fun for you. It has brought back many, many memories of places we've visited and things we enjoyed doing, that didn't necessarily fit into any of our other chapters. To "scatter-shoot," as we have done here, was like a game of "can you remember when ..." and so I close this chapter with a little game.

Call it Texas trivia. Remember the cartoon character Alley Oop,

Popeye has a prominent place in front of City Hall in Crystal City.

back in "Ira-Ann"? Well, where would you go to find another famous cartoon character, Popeye? The answer is Crystal City, in Zavala County.

Now the town of Crystal City has a lot of things they're proud of—oil, great hunting and fishing—but the one thing they are most proud of is that they are the self-proclaimed Spinach Capital of the World. And rightfully so. As you approach Crystal City, you are surrounded by great fields of spinach and signs by such canning companies as Del Monte that pretty well tell you that this is spinach country. There's even a sign promoting the annual Spinach Festival. And if you go to the City Hall in downtown Crystal City, you'll find the statue of Popeye, the loveable seafaring cartoon character who loves his spinach, standing tall in the Spinach Capital of the World.

From Alley Oop to Popeye ... how's that for scatter-shooting? ✪

Almost every city, town or community had a welcome sign.

260

CHAPTER ELEVEN

Signs

*N*o one could have ever convinced Linda or I when we started on this tour of Texas towns that we would become amused or entertained by signs. Yes, signs. Old advertising signs. Unique signs of places and things. Signs with misspelled words. There were even signs that provided some philosophy or lessons for life.

At first, they were just hand-written signs with maybe a misspelled word or two. Then we got hooked on the idea of looking for odd or unusual signs. And finally, we began to photograph them. By the time our tour of Texas was over, we had collected untold photographs of nothing but signs.

Some signs just begged to be photographed.

For example, in Palo Pinto, county seat of picturesque Palo Pinto County, the old county jail is now a museum. On the front door of the old county jail, just behind a cactus plant, someone had taken an old weathered board and burned into the wood: "Museum Open, June – August, Saturday & Sunday, 2 to 4 a.m." Then there were two telephone numbers listed for appointments or tours. Now folks, regardless of how great this museum might be, they might get a few lookers being open on just Saturdays and Sundays, if only for three months during the summer, but I doubt there will be a bunch of callers for tours between 2 and 4 a.m. in the morning.

Typos are one thing; telling the truth is sometimes stranger than fiction.

As we drove into Olney in Young County, known for its dove, quail and white-tailed deer during the hunting seasons, there was a large banner that stretched across the highway welcoming visitors. Well, more than just visitors. It read: "Welcome One-Arm Dove Hunters." Now, at first glance, I figured someone was just having a little sick humor about dove hunters not being too safety-minded. Otherwise, can you imagine someone creating a special dove hunt just for one-arm sportsmen? Yep, that's exactly what it was. There was a special competition that weekend for one-armed folks who enjoy hunting, too.

Welcome sign in Olney wasn't a joke.

WE HAD TRAVELED many times to Meridian, near Lake Whitney in Bosque County, even before we began our grand tour of Texas, and always enjoyed a great lunch at Henry's, a rather large restaurant and always busy. On this particular day, we were eager to get a bite at

Henry's, but were surprised to see a sign written on butcher paper with a black marker, taped to the front door. It read: "Due to lack of help for graduation, Henry's will be closing at 2:30 Friday, May 22. We will be open Saturday at 7 a.m."

The message was simple: Meridian is a family town, and when they're having high school graduation, there are a lot more people who want to go to graduation ceremonies than want to work or eat, so Henry's just shut down like it was a national holiday. It was definitely a celebrated holiday in Meridian.

Some signs bring back old memories.

We were on Farm Road 542 at Texas Hwy. 7 in the rolling Trinity River bottoms of Leon County, near Sweet Oak, when we came across a sign on a

From
Linda's notes

Leon County — The old courthouse and jail at Centerville has undergone some great restoration. ...On Farm Road 977, we were surprised to see lions, baboons, monkeys, sheep, ducks, ostrich, goats and tigers near the Two Mile Methodist Church and cemetery. ...At the Old Bowling Cemetery, three graves have chairs beside them. All three buried there died on the same date. ...Jewitt has Indoor Trade Day every second Saturday, held in its Civic Center.

Old faded "Cutter Bill" sign in Leon County brought back memories.

fence line that brought back a lot of memories for me. The sign was so rusted it was hard to read, but it had a picture of a horse head. Above the horse head, there were the near-indistinguishable words, "Cauble Ranch," and under it, "Registered Quarter Horses. Home of Cutter Bill."

Some of you old-timers may remember Cutter Bill, one of the all-time great cutting horses. In fact, Rex Cauble, who owned the Cauble Ranch, opened a very upscale ranch store in Dallas many years ago named Cutter Bill's, which is now closed. Some of you who travel between Dallas and Denton may remember a very picturesque barn and stables that had Cauble Ranch on the top of the barn, which was then the home of Cutter Bill. But the old rusty sign in Leon County marked what was Cutter Bill's original home, and it was very sentimental to find it along our travels.

From
Linda's notes

Rusk County — The East Texas Oil Boom began in Henderson when the Daisy Bradford No. 3 oil well blew in 1930, after three years of failed attempts to strike oil. The site is marked by a granite stone a mile north of Pioneer Park, which features derrick-covered picnic pavilions. ...The world's largest lignite-fired electric power generating plant is located at Henderson. ...The monument in front of the new school in New London, in memory of the 311 students and teachers killed by a gas explosion in 1937, is awesome. ...Near Laneville, an old church built in 1873 was bought by trustees at auction and it is used for special events.

DO I HAVE A FAVORITE? Well, yes I do.

There's an old antique and junk store in the deep East Texas town of Mount Enterprise, Rusk County, that looks about as old as most of its wares. There was a lock on the front door, and a sign that said it was closed—and yet, there was a lot of old merchandise out on the lawn in front of the store, the kind you just wouldn't want to bring indoors every night. And there was another sign, this one hand-scrawled with red paint on a piece of wood nailed just above the front door. It read: "What you take while I'm away, it's you and God on Judgment Day."

Oh, yeah ... there didn't seem to be a single piece of junk missing from that front yard.

That old sign, and many more, got our attention, and made for a few fun photos, some of which are

Sign in Mount Pleasant says junk in front yard not all junk.

included here for a giggle or a guffaw. It's all part of seeing Texas on the back roads, where looking for unique signs can be as much fun as reading Burma Shave jingles along the way. ✪

In Carson County, a longer ironing board is needed.

Blue Bell country is everywhere.

Dated Dr Pepper sign in Venus, before they dropped the dot after Dr.

266

Post Office sign in Maryneal: When you get to age 90, being there is gift enough.

In Wood County, if you buy a storm cellar, can you move it?

Thoughts from Garwood sign gets A-Plus grade!

Welcome sign in Milford tells it like it is.

Sign in Castell, Llano County: for English-speaking folks only?

Welcome to Red Springs: Turn right, if you can read this sign.

In Frisco, Collin County, Half Main is halfway to Main.

Scurry County sign shows the art of farming is a proud tradition.

Is Kaufman County cemetery also closed to ghosts?

Welcome sign to Happy, Swisher County, will bring a smile or two.

For milk, bread or eggs, come in; for lottery tickets, honk.

In Rhonesboro, does population figure include all the possums?

His and hers, but not theirs, in Brownfield.

Major Golden event, but held every Oct. 21-22?

Who remembers this tonic? Well, they had to call it something.

274

Raise your hand if you ever rolled your own.

Nickel parking gets a customer in Nacogdoches.

Faded memories in Kingsville.

Window into yesteryear in Shackleford County.

Rainbow was the bread in the good old days!

In Brazoria County, the Baptists stick together.

You don't park in front of a bank and start taking photos.

CHAPTER TWELVE

Trouble Along The Way

There is a good reason they call Texas "the friendly state." It is unbelievable how nice people were to us as we traveled 135,000 miles across this big state.

Of course, folks were curious when we came to their town. Even when we caused some concern among suspecting folks—like taking pictures of banks—we never met anyone we didn't like, even though it may not have been smooth-going at the outset.

As you might suspect, one doesn't travel for three and a half years to every nook, cranny and crook in the road in Texas and not experience trouble along the way. Even so, for every so-called problem we faced, we met great people and came away with a very positive experience.

Some of our "troubles" were, admittedly afterwards, amusing. We have already described some of those moments—like the time we were in Wolfe City on Main Street, taking photographs, and the bank just happened to be on the corner. Yep, someone thought we were casing the joint and they called the police.

Of course, that got cleared up, as did the time we were in Graford and wanted to take photos of the local bank's brass teller cages. Yes, we know you don't walk into a bank to take photographs, but even trying to get a good sight of the brass teller cages by driving slowly in front of a bank three or four times will get the defensive adrenaline of suspicion going.

In that case, it was the mayor on his riding lawn mower who blocked our way, then led us straight to the bank, where we got our pictures and had a great time visiting with the bank president. It would never have worked out that well for us if it wasn't for the friendly folks in Graford and all the other wonderful places we visited in our travels through Texas.

SOME "TROUBLES" WERE, in hindsight, minor compared to some other troubles we experienced. One was a wreck—not a minor happening as it turned out.

A young lady pulled out from a stop sign in Uvalde and hit our Suburban in the right rear. We spun around, crashed into the curb, and Linda was pretty shaken when we came to a screeching stop. We escaped any serious injury, but the Suburban didn't. It was heavily damaged, front and back, left-side and right-side.

When we had our wreck, it was really a wreck!

More battle scars on our Suburban.

The police arrived and were very courteous. They called a wrecker, and when it arrived, the wrecker driver offered to call us a taxi cab. Well, being from the Big City (at that time, Big D), I began to think everyone here is in cahoots, and they're going to get their brother or uncle in the act, and ... but, no sir. I was somewhat surprised when we arrived at the auto dealership where our Suburban was to be taken for overhaul, and told there would be no charge for the taxi ride. It was just a courtesy thing.

We called our good friends in Uvalde, George and Ginger Cooper, who own the Spanish Dagger Hunting Resort, just outside of Uvalde, and they just happened to be home. They drove into town, picked us up, and loaned us a vehicle to use until we could get our business in Uvalde taken care of.

The young man who was foreman of the body shop took great pains with our vehicle—there was extensive front and back damage, all four tires had to be replaced—and he even helped arrange to get us a rent car, since we were a six-hour drive from home.

When the Suburban was ready two weeks later, and all the insurance claims and approvals had been inked, the shop foreman called and offered to meet us halfway to Dallas to deliver our vehicle. In fact, after a long day at work, he and his wife drove our Suburban to Temple, spent the night there, then returned to Uvalde with the rent car we had been using—all to make life easier for us. It was another one of those unbelievable goodwill gestures that we found throughout our travels.

WE WERE IN MULESHOE, out in Bailey County, and getting ready to leave when we found our car battery deader than, well, road kill on U.S. 84. It was a Sunday, and we knew it was going to be difficult to find a place to get help—much less a new battery. But the motel folks gave us a name, we called, they came out, gave our dead battery a jump-start, then followed us to an auto parts place that was open. And the first thing we knew we were back on the road. Even a couple waiting to get service asked that we be put ahead on the wait list, because "we were visitors." Now, where else in this great country of ours do visitors get that kind of treatment?

OKAY, SO MULESHOE is a b-i-g small town (population 4,453) in what is mostly big farm country. But what if you had troubles in a place

From Linda's notes

Bailey County — While in Muleshoe, we visited with Rusty Whitt, his wife and mother, and their hard-working crew harvesting corn. Joined them and their working "hands" eating home-made chicken-fried steak (with all the trimmings) out of the back of a pick-up truck. ... Magann Rennels owns and runs the local Channel 6 out of her home, featuring local news and happenings. A TV camera is mounted on a turntable, which she can swing around to take video of still pictures, thus offering local businesses "TV" advertising at affordable prices. ... She has two mail boxes, one for personal letters, the other for Channel 6 items. There's also a note from Magann not to drop obits in the Channel 6 box, but to place them under the door so she can get to them "sooner."

Our dead battery in Muleshoe was as lifeless as this mule statue.

where a Resume Speed sign wasn't within miles?

Welcome to Placid (population 32), near the center of Texas, off U.S. 377 in McCulloch County. It was getting to be sundown, in a

Don't have a flat in Placid when all stores in town are closed. We did.

town without a paved road, and its only two stores were closed. That was when I discovered my right rear tire was flat. Oh, did I say it was another Sunday?

Needless to say, I'm not a great fan of jacking up cars—especially Suburban carryalls that are loaded to the gills with gear, and a jack buried under it all. Nonetheless, I got out and surveyed the situation. About 50 yards from us, there were some folks coming out of a house

that appeared to be "company" leaving. Linda offered to walk down the road, thinking that there might be someone who had a jack more accessible than ours.

As it turned out, one of the men had a long-handled, hydraulic big-time jack—far more macho than the toy-size jack they put into cars nowadays. Not only did he provide the jack, but he did all the work—from jacking up the Suburban, taking the tire off, and replacing it with the spare (also under a ton of travel stuff). Hallelujah! And to think I was concerned about being in a place where I didn't know anyone, in a place that seemed to be closed for the day, and facing darkness in a dark moment.

IN TEXAS, FRIENDLINESS is not a myth, and more than a motto. And it can show up at the dangest moment.

We were in Victoria, one of the first three towns to be incorporated by the Republic of Texas, now a city over 61,000, and visiting the McFadden Ranch when a gold cap came off one of my teeth. Now, that's a scary thing for me. There was no pain when I discovered the loose cap, but the thought there *might* be pain was painful enough. Or maybe it was just the thought of having to go see a dentist.

Anyway, we drove back to town to see if we could find a dentist office. We stopped at a quick-

From
Linda's notes

McCulloch County — Brady has an old jail, converted to a museum. ... The Texas Muzzle Loaders Rifle Association is based in Brady, with "shoots" in Feb., June and Oct. in full costume. ... Have your camera ready when you visit Camp San Saba. A photo opportunity is everywhere you turn. ... Ruins of an old ball field with rock walls and ticket cages is in Doole. The largest graduating class in Doole was 14. ... A marker between Placid and Mercury claims to be the geographic center of Texas.

We ate lunch at the McFadden Cafe when—oops—a cap came off a tooth!

shop service station to check the Yellow Pages, and a girl working there said her dentist was just a few blocks away. Being mid-day, we went to the dentist office just as the dentist was coming back from lunch. He took me in—no appointment, mind you—and had the cap fitted and back in place in less than 30 minutes, at a very nominal charge.

Now some may say that's pure luck. Maybe so, but it was another case of trouble along the way that ended with a happy ending, and a chance to be the recipient of good ol' Texas hospitality. Even in a dentist's chair.

FOLKS TRAVELING TEXAS, if they encounter trouble on the road, will most likely find down-home hospitality at a gas station outpost. I've always said that some of Texas' most hospitable heroes are our friendly, dedicated auto mechanics.

Our favorite mechanic lives in Seguin. We found him after our Suburban began sputtering after we gassed up in Floresville, county seat of Wilson County, for the second time in two days. We had found

Seguin is also the home of our favorite mechanic.

an old gas station, barely making it financially, just as our gas tank was nearing empty for the first time, then again two days later. The station's only gas pump was a dandy. It was an oldie, and as slow as molasses in Vermont. Eager to get down the road, it seemed like it took an hour to pump a gallon of gas—so filling a 21-gallon empty tank seemed like an all-day affair.

After finally filling up, we headed west on Texas 97 for the Promised Land Dairy, home to the largest Jersey herd in the world, and producer of some of the most heavenly ice cream this side of Brenham. En

289

From
Linda's notes

Victoria County — The memorial square in Victoria includes an old bandstand and graves of pioneers, plus a historic wind-driven gristmill which ground corn for German farmers before the Civil War. ...Downtown McFadden would make a great movie set. Nothing has been restored. ...The Infant Jesus of Prague Catholic Church is the only privately-owned Catholic Church in the U.S. ...Signs throughout Inez have Bible verses printed on them.

route, the engine started to sputter, like there was a timing or electrical problem. It would chug in spurts, then purr like a pussy cat. Chug, purr. Chug, purr.

After leaving the Promised Land, headed for Seguin, the engine started acting up again. We began looking for a garage or service station, stopping at two backyard fix-it shops. Both mechanics said up front they didn't have the right equipment to check out the fuel system properly. Fortunately, we were able to hobble into Seguin, and found a local Chevrolet dealership in the downtown area. It was, of course, late in the day.

The mechanic dutifully pulled the carburetor, cleaned out the filter system, blew out the gas line, and everything else he could think of, and nothing seemed to help. So the mechanic said he needed to pull the gas tank. Now this

From the Promise Land Dairy, we sputtered all the way to Seguin with an ailing car.

is a major ordeal, and it was near quitting time. But our faithful mechanic refused to quit. When he took the gas tank off, and cleaned it out, he found a tremendous amount of rust—which no doubt came from the old service station pump in Floresville.

I half-expected the mechanic to suggest that we find a motel, that he would finish the job the next morning, but he didn't. He worked some three hours past his normal quitting time to make sure our problem was fixed and to get us back on the road.

Of course, while our mechanic worked, we talked a lot about our tour of Texas, the interesting places we had been, and great people we had met. And we added him to our ever-lengthening list of people who helped turn a negative situation into a positive experience.

IN RETROSPECT, maybe the best thing that happened—thinking positive about a negative situation while traveling the back roads—is that I still have a wife named Linda. No, it isn't what you might think.

What is the one thing that you never plan on happening when you're on the road? Well, yes, you do worry about such things as running out of gas, or getting a flat tire in the middle of nowhere, or getting into an accident.

But you never think about having a heart attack.

It happened, in just about the most remote corner of Texas.

We were out at the old Fort Leaton State Historic Site, on FM Road 170, on the Mexico border just west of Presidio, when Linda said she was out of breath and could hardly walk, and returned to the car. As you know, this is Big Bend country—mountain country in Texas—and I thought maybe the rugged, higher elevation was getting to her.

It was late in the day, so we drove back to Alpine,

From Linda's notes

Wilson County — Floresville holds its annual Peanut Festival in October. ...Buildings around the Wilson County courthouse need to be restored. ...The Promised Land Dairy, just outside of Floresville, has a petting zoo, miniature golf and an ice cream parlor/ restaurant.

We thought it was high altitude at Fort Leaton (above) when Linda had breathing difficulties. Four days later, she underwent bypass surgery.

not exactly a skip and a jump (about 90 miles), to spend the night. The next morning, as we loaded the Suburban, Linda once again said she was out of breath, and could hardly breathe. We talked about her problem on the way back home, and I had her promise me she would

see her doctor that very next Monday morning.

Reluctantly, she did. It was only when I got a call from Dr. Mike McCullough that morning—telling me to get Linda at his office, that she would not be allowed to drive to Baylor Hospital for a visit with the cardiologist—that I realized how serious the problem was. Two days later, she had four bypasses.

We were lucky. Linda was lucky. Linda was lucky that it was not as severe as it could have been. We were both lucky that we were able to drive home and get back to our own familiar surroundings, to our own doctors, and get the situation corrected.

One hundred and thirty-five thousand miles. Three and one-half years of checking out 3,300 towns. And some that weren't.

One wreck. One dead battery. One flat tire. One heart attack.

Things can happen when you're traveling the backroads of Texas. But if you do encounter trouble, you're in good hands, thanks to the generosity and graciousness of the most friendly people you will ever meet along the way. ✪

Towering 67 feet high, a 30-ton Sam Houston looms over I-45 near Huntsville, the world's tallest statue of an American hero.

CHAPTER THIRTEEN

Photos, Photos, Photos

We always took two cameras on our trips through Texas. The reason was simple. We started out with one camera, and the battery died. That can be a killer if you want to document your visit to, say, Whiteflat, Dot, Gunsight, Prairie Dell—you name it, all those interesting out-of-the-way places in this state.

One of our goals was to "capture" by camera interesting places we visited, or unique things we saw, or old bygone-era structures that might not be left for others to enjoy. And as we traveled, we categorized our photographs by counties—254 categories in all.

When we began to get serious about this book, we re-categorized these photos. That was no small task. As you might guess, we have thousands upon thousands of photographs. I now know we took well over 21,000. We have since eliminated over 1,000—those photographs that were out of focus, too light, too dark, duplications, and so on. There were some, of course, that I couldn't even remember why I took it.

We have now re-filed some 20,000 photos into two categories—First Team and Second-Team. Our "second-team" photos are those that may never again see the light of day, but could be useful if we need to refresh a memory or do some future research. Our "first team" photos are those we felt were important enough to be considered for this book, and—God willing—future books that we might do.

We then took our First Team photos and categorized them into various subjects—much like we have done for this publication. I would say we have between 8,500 and 9,000 photographs in our "first-team" categories. Of course, we're only able to share just a few of these with you. We could do a full book of photographs just on country churches and cemeteries—over 2,000 just in those two categories. Ditto for old post offices, courthouses, old jails, school houses, and on and on.

Going through all of these photos has helped us recall so many stories and memories that our notes may have missed. Following are three anecdotes involving our photo-taking adventure.

OLD BANKS IN TEXAS never die. They just change their names from time to time. But regardless of their name, whether it's First National Bank of Chillicothe, or just "The Bank" in Milford, you don't just walk in—or even drive by—and start taking photographs. Banks are

The bank in Graford had brass teller windows.

naturally a bit nervous about that sort of thing.

We were taking photos of Main Street in Wolfe City, and of course the bank was on the corner. The bank folks didn't know who we were, and no doubt thought we were casing the joint. And so they called the police.

But that wasn't the only time we raised an eyebrow or two in our travels, thanks to the local friendly bank. There was one bank we heard about in Graford, Palo Pinto County, that just begged for a photograph. Graford is a small town not too many resume speed signs northwest of Mineral Wells, and the town's only bank was 90 years old. We heard that it had brass teller cage windows. Naturally, Linda thought how neat it would be to take some photos of those brass teller windows. I told her you don't just walk in a bank and start taking pictures, that we needed a plan.

We drove slowly past this bank—about three times, I think—and kept making a loop around the center of town. As we came around a corner on our fourth pass, a heavy-set gentleman on a riding lawn mower cut us off at a stop sign. Yes, a riding mower!

He then called out "Just who are you?" And naturally I asked: "Well, who are you?" And he said, in a rather dignified drawl, "Well, I'm the mayor of this town, and the mayor pro tem is on that other lawn mower. We just happened to be mowing at the community center, saw you all driving by real slow like, and we just wondered what you people are up to."

We introduced ourselves, told him why we were driving slow by the bank, and—this could only happen in Texas, folks—he then escorted us, on his lawn mower, to the bank, took us into the

From Linda's notes

Hunt County — I was raised in Greenville ...Hunt County was (and still is) known for its rich black waxy soil. ...Also from in Hunt County, near Kingston, was World War II hero and film star Audie Murphy, America's most decorated soldier, who starred in a movie about himself, "To Hell and Back." ...There is a historical marker at Kingston, just north of Greenville, for the Shields brothers who traveled with the Barnum & Bailey Circus as 7-foot giants. ...Commerce is the home of Texas A&M University at Commerce, but was East Texas State Teachers College when I went there.

bank, and introduced us to the president of the bank. And we have some great photos of the inside of that bank, and those brass teller cages we heard about.

ON ONE BEAUTIFUL SUNNY afternoon, probably around 2 o'clock, we were heading out of the little town of O'Donnell, on the Dawson and Lynn County line. O'Donnell is the boyhood home of Dan Blocker, alias "Hoss Cartwright" of the long-time TV western series *Bonanza*. As we drove north on Farm-to-Market Road 1054 in Lynn County,

A 30-year flying veteran, Sam Pridmore makes a low-flying spray run over a field in Lynn County.

everywhere we looked we saw maybe eight or ten crop-duster aircraft flying high and low over the sprawling cotton fields. I had never seen that many crop dusters at one time. They were not dangerously close to each other, and in fact were miles apart, but we pulled off on the side of the road just to watch these dare-devil pilots do their job.

It was like a side show. It was definitely a rural version of an air show. It was amazing to see how

these bulky-looking aircraft could maneuver in the air, rising quickly into the cloudless sky like an eagle, then swooping down and low over the flat table-top terrain as if to catch a scampering jack rabbit. They weren't hunting jack rabbits, of course, but were spraying the fields with chemicals to help the cotton and grain sorghum crops grow, or to keep down those pesky pests that like to feast on the tender leaves of young crops.

As we marveled at the talent of these "farmer pilots," we noticed that two of them seemed to be working together. We wanted to get closer, so we turned right onto FM Road 1313, toward the community of Grassland, where these two crop dusters were working this one section of land. One would make a pass, then head up several hundred feet into the sky. As the first pilot banked to the left to circle back, the second pilot would make his low

From Linda's notes

Palo Pinto County — Oh, those beautiful rolling hills of Palo Pinto County! ...Discovery of "medicinal qualities" in its water made Mineral Wells nationally famous in 1885. Early claims boasted that waters of the so-called Crazy Well could cure mental illness and other maladies. ...The old Baker Hotel in Mineral Wells is still the city's downtown icon, yet it has remained empty for many years. It was once a well-traveled health spa resort hotel, catering to the inflicted as well as the rich. ...J&J Restaurant & Feed Store in the Brazos community is a great place for hamburgers and home-made pies. They "feed" you well! ...The Jackson Grocery in Santo has an old soda fountain still in use. ...Tommy Michaels was the president of the First National Bank in Graford when we stopped to see the old-time brass teller cages.

"spray" run. It became obvious that they were somehow keeping track of where each had made their last run.

Looking up the road a ways, I spotted a pick-up truck with five-foot poles that had flags flapping in the breeze. Each time a crop duster would come down over an area, the man in the truck would pull his vehicle forward a bit and the next pilot would head directly at the truck with the flags. We later learned the man on the ground was the "flag man"—the key to helping the crop dusters know where they had to spray next.

We also noticed there were power lines along the side of the road as we watched the crop dusters work, which of course added to the day-time drama. The crop dusters would fly low over the fields, release their chemicals, then with a roar of their powerful engine would pull almost straight up to miss the electrified lines along the road. It was fascinating. The aircraft would almost stall as it climbed straight up, then catch its mechanical breath, bank and circle back. Again and again.

I told Linda that I just had to photograph this scene. She said "James, you're crazy. They may crash. You just stay out of their way!" But I boldly said "No, Linda, I've just got to do it."

I walked over to the flag man and told him what I wanted to do. He nodded, keeping a closer watch on his two flying buddies than on me. And then I stepped out into the cotton field to catch the next fly-by. Now, in retrospect, I have to admit this was not a very intelligent decision. I was probably only 50 feet from the electrical lines I had observed before. I told myself that if these pilots performed their duties properly, I'd be okay. After all, they had managed to miss the electric lines all the time we had been watching. Plus, I figured, the electric lines would protect me from any total disaster.

I got down on my knees, not to pray but to put on my zoom lens, and focused on an aircraft as it sped low over the cotton field furrows. I did this for several runs to get the feel for what it might take to get a good picture, moving to my left each time a crop duster would make another pass. Now, I thought, I was ready for the Big Shot.

My chance came. I aligned myself so that the next aircraft headed straight at me, no more than 10 feet off the ground. Sure enough, just as it seemed the aircraft was right on me, I snapped the shutter just before the pilot pulled back on his stick and coaxed his craft upwards toward the heavens—not to miss me, but to miss the power lines. I repeated the same scenario with the second plane, hoping that I had focused properly with my zoom lens as it flew in low, then rose sharply.

I got the name of one pilot, Sam Pridmore, who happened to be the man in charge. And in fact, it was the Pridmore Aerial Spraying Company that was working the fields that day. I also got his phone number. After we processed the film back home, I was delighted to see I had taken one of my favorite photographs during our tour of Texas!

Figuring that Sam Pridmore might like to have a copy of the photo I had taken of his fly-by that afternoon in Lynn County, I called and left a message on his recorder. The next day, I got a call from a lady who was Sam Pridmore's wife. She was calling from the hospital in Tahoka where she worked, and she said she would really like to have a photo, since Sam had been a crop duster for over 30 years and he did not have a single photo of himself or any of his aircraft in action and spraying! I sent him an 8x10 glossy print.

Shortly thereafter, I got another call, again from Mrs. Pridmore, who said she would pay for having the photo blown up to 11x14 so it could hang over their fireplace. She wanted to give it to her husband as a Christmas present. Needless

From
Linda's notes

O'Donnell — A statue of Dan Blocker, TV's "Hoss Cartwright" of *Bonanza* fame, adorns a park across from an old two-story former bank building (circa 1925) in O'Donnell, which sits on the Lynn-Dawson county line. ...The town's old bank now houses the O'Donnell Museum featuring a "Blockerbilia" exhibit along with an old telephone system, organ, a blacksmith shop, school room, post office, lawyer and doctor offices. Museum is open Tuesday through Saturday, but closed for lunch. ...Dan Blocker grew up in O'Donnell, but was born in Bowie County. ...There is no 19th century history to O'Donnell. It was founded by the Panhandle & Santa Fe Railroad in 1908, and like many little towns in Texas, named for a railroad official.

to say, I didn't charge her for the cost of getting an 11x14 print, since I was so complimented by the fact someone else liked my photograph that much! It was also a thrill that I survived the experience in the first place—having ignored Linda's warning that I might get myself killed just to get the picture of a lifetime!

ON ONE OF OUR TRIPS to Big Bend country, the Annual Cowboy Poets Gathering was under way in Alpine. It's a big event that happens the first of March every year. On this particular Saturday morning, we were invited to a chuck wagon breakfast. It was well attended, not only by the cowboy poets themselves like Red Stegall, but by well-known western artists, country-and-western stars and the like.

At such chuck wagon feeds, the cooking is done on the ground—from camp coffee made in big metal pots hanging over a crackling wood fire and loaded with coffee grounds, to make-shift griddles where flapjacks bubble in the grease, to huge cast-iron frying pans where bacon sizzles over the open fire. I still drool just thinking about it. It was such an authentic cowboy scene—not exactly how you might picture cooking at home—that I knew it had to be "captured" on film.

There happened to be a pick-up truck not too far from the campfire scene where the bacon was sizzling, and I got up in the pick-up bed to take a photograph. I knew it was a photograph that spoke of the Old West, but I also knew that it didn't capture the aroma of the fire-kissed flapjacks, or the grease-sizzling bacon, or the eye-opening waft of camp coffee. But when I began to show the photograph to others, they all said it should be entered in a photo contest.

Now, I don't know all the where's-and-what-for's that make for a good photo. But folks said it had everything that makes a good photo great, from the early morning light to the glow of the campfires. So when the State Fair of Texas opened its annual 15-day run in Dallas in early October, I took my photo of the cowboy cookout with me to see if I might enter it into the state fair's photo competition. I talked with some people who seemed to be in charge, and they agreed to give me an idea of whether I should enter it or not. "By all means, enter it!" they both exclaimed. So I did, in an appropriate category, as an amateur.

I don't think I've been so shocked in my life as I was when I received a call from someone with the State Fair of Texas, telling me that my photograph had won first place in its class! So as you might guess, it is now framed, there's a blue ribbon hanging on it, and it is another one of those "great memories" of our unique travels through Texas.

WE'VE TITLED THIS CHAPTER Photos, Photos, Photos for a reason. We wanted to share some photos we took throughout this state that didn't exactly win blue ribbon awards, or fit into the categories we picked for this book like churches, cemeteries, signs and such. To wrap up our tour of Texas towns, we have selected just a few out of the thousands we have in our files of places we went, people we met, and points of interest we visited to share with you, in hopes you find that they also strike a memory cord with you. Each photograph conjures up a memory for both Linda and I, and we hope they might for you—or at least be pleasing to look at.

Following are a few snapshots of our wonderful State of Texas, taken at a time when life is going by too fast, where yesterday is but a memory, today is now yesterday, and tomorrow is today. Don't let too many tomorrows go by before you get off the hectic highways and get on the backroads of Texas. We plan to keep traveling to see a little bit more of yesterday that has helped make today a brighter tomorrow. And we will always bring along two cameras to make sure we don't miss a thing! ✪

Heading north on U.S. 83 in Hemphill County, we followed a trailer of horses when ...

... we crested the hill, only to come face to face with this sheet-metal dinosaur!

The post office at Shafter in Big Bend country.

One of our favorite photos of old school houses, this one in Whiteflat.

305

A rails-to-trails tunnel in the Caprock State Park, south of Quitaque.

City Hall in Paint Rock, Concho County.

The Last Chance Saloon, Lipscomb County, kept upright by a tree.

City Hall in Abbott, Hill County.

Masonic Lodge and First Baptist Church in Kildare, Cass County.

A beautiful old Masonic Lodge in Greenwood, Wise County.

Old theater used in The Last Picture Show, *in Archer City, Archer County.*

309

"Texas" is the No. 1 name for theaters in Texas, like this one in San Angelo.

The 1855 Seward Plantation home in Washington County.

A Texas Panhandle windmill near the Boot Leg community, Deaf Smith County.

The Governor's Mansion in Austin.

Old Victorian home in Crockett, one of thousands found in our travels through Texas.

A ranch gate near Camp San Saba, McCullouch County.

The old Bulah School and playground in Cherokee County.

A tanker heads for harbor near Corpus Christi.

The state-operated Lynchburg Ferry near Houston.

Cowboy cooking at the Big Bend Saddlery Breakfast at Alpine in the Big Bend area.

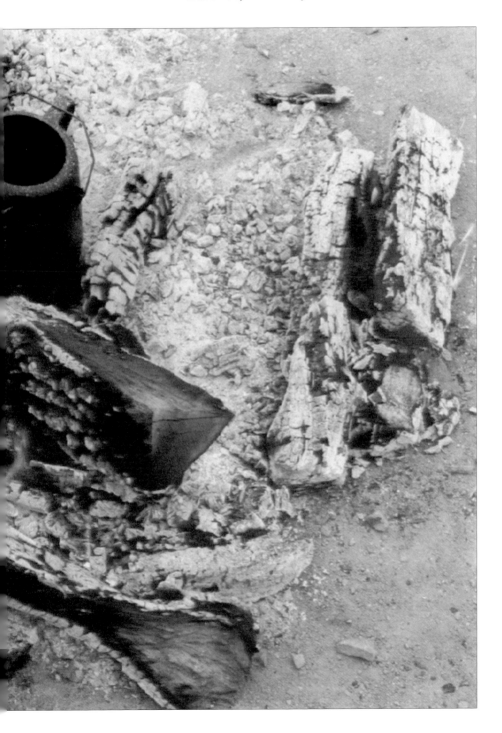

A mare and her colt in Stonewall County.

A cow and her calf in Clay County.

Cornudas Cafe tables, dressed in jeans and boots, make it a favorite stop for truckers in Hudspeth County.

The 1913 Walburg State Bank in Williamson County is a survivor of the Great Depression.

Original headquarters of the famed XIT Ranch near Channing, Hartley County.

Newly-renovated depot in Brady, McCulloch County.

An 1893 general store in Neches, Anderson County.

Abandoned gas station in Red River County.

An old ice house in Albany was a rare find.

San Jose Mission in San Antonio.

It was here at Fort Parker in 1836, that Comanche Indians stormed the fort and captured nine-year-old Cynthia Ann Parker. She became "Indianized," as they called it back then, marrying a Comanche chief and giving birth to three children, including Quanah Parker.

Cemetery at Fort Parker Memorial Park was started in 1836 after the infamous Indian raid that year killed five members of the Parker family .

Welcome, and remember, "don't mess with Texas."

An iron and wood bridge in old Fort Griffin.

and
The Roads of Texas Continue...